WAR
WITH
EMPTY HANDS

Self-Defense
Against Aggression

LENOX CRAMER

WAR
WITH
EMPTY HANDS

Self-Defense
Against Aggression

ALPHA PUBLICATIONS
SHARON CENTER, OHIO

WAR WITH EMPTY HANDS
Self-Defense Against Aggression
by Lenox Cramer
Copyright © 1986 by Alpha Publications of Ohio

ISBN 0-939427-41-9
Printed in the United States of America

Published by Alpha Publications of Ohio
P.O. Box 308
Sharon Center, Ohio 44274 USA

Photos by Victoria Richards
Models: Vida Djukic
        Mike Brkic
        Zarko Stojanovic
        Charles R. Bromton

Jacket illustration and design by
Alpha Publications of Ohio © 1986, 1991.

Contents

PART TWO

DISCLAIMER

The author and publisher of this instructional book are not responsible in any manner for any injury which may occur as a result of reading and/or following the instructions contained herein.

It is essential that before following any of the activities herein described, the reader should first consult his physician.

About the Author

Lenox Cramer has a vast and valuable knowledge of the Martial Arts and has refined this talent into one of the fastest, deadliest, and easiest to learn forms of self-defense known! His methods have been tried and proven on "some of the most violent streets" in America, as well as in the deadly jungles of Southeast Asia.

Starting out with Judo at age 12 in a YMCA located in a tough inner city, he attained 1st degree brown belt ranking before enlisting in the U.S. Army at age 17. During the following years he studied the Korean military style of karate taught at Fort Bragg, N.C., Japanese Shotokan, and Japanese Zendokan Ryu Karate Do, which has *no* sporting aspect. This form of karate retains its Warrior roots and teaches strictly combat-applicable technique and strategies. Cramer attained a 3rd degree black belt with the Zendokan Budokai of America and ran two schools for the ZBA as Chief Instructor. His title in the ZBA organization translates to "Warrior Monk". He also served as Chief Instructor in the hand-to-hand/close combat course for Sunshine Security International for two years. Lenox Cramer has a B.A. in philosophy from the University of South Florida which has helped him translate this potent form of martial arts to his readers.

Lenox Cramer served his country proudly, beginning with the 3rd Battalion, 173rd Airborne Brigade, and then volunteered for their Long Range Recon Patrol (LRRP) element (which was later consolidated into the infamous 75th Rangers). He was Airborne/Ranger qualified prior to his first tour of duty in Vietnam, which lasted from 1967 to 1968. Lenox Cramer was one of nine suvivors of a base camp that was overrun in the fierce fighting of the 1968 Tet Offensive. He states, "Martial arts training should be the basis for every infantryman's/woman's training. It provides the self-confidence needed to sustain a soldier (or civilian) in combat at close quarters." Further, "I've seen GI's freeze when the Cong ran through their lines and the fighting went hand-to-hand, the M-16's jammed, and the time too tight for drawing side arms. Karate could have saved them."

Upon the completion of his first tour in Vietnam, he was stationed at Fort Bragg, N.C. with the 82nd Airborne Division, but quickly volunteered for Special Forces training. He graduated the Special Warfare Center there and returned to Southeast Asia with the 5th Special Forces Group in July, 1969, having traded his beloved and well-earned Ranger black beret for his new Special Forces green beret. After volunteering for recon duty with this elite group, he went through their Recondo training facility at Nha Trang and was posted to Project Delta, an in-country LRRP unit. From there he went on to the Military Assistance Command Vietnam/Studies and Observations Group (MAC-V SOG) to further ''fine tune'' his martial art skills on cross border LRRP and search and destroy missions into the denied areas of Laos and North Vietnam.

Lenox Cramer served a total of 2½ years of duty in Southeast Asia, earning the Distinguished Service Cross, Silver Star, Bronze Star, and numerous Purple Hearts.

Foreword

When one of Lenox Cramer's case officers in Vietnam who also knows **War with Empty Hands,** was on a covert operation in Beirut, Lebanon, several Druse militia men tried to capture him inside his hotel room. They were armed with various weapons, including one firearm. This former U.S. Intelligence officer killed three of his attackers with his bare hands using the same self-defense fighting techniques that are taught in this book, and survived to tell about it!

Whether the fight is on the streets of Attackersville, U.S.A., the brutal jungles of Southeast Asia, the equally brutal jungles of South America, or a hotel room in Beirut, these self-defense methods have been used and tested under *REAL* battlefield conditions successfully! It is the true desire of the author, his warrior comrades, and the publisher that if you or your loved ones are ever confronted by a violent attacker that *War with Empty Hands* will give you the assurance that you are capable of protecting yourself and your loved ones in life threatening situations, as well as the tools to do so!

PART ONE
Chapter One

A History

Hand-to-hand combat is as old as the human race. The different methods of fighting that prevailed in different parts of the world took generations to evolve and are still in the process of change today. Nothing is static, nothing stops growing or it dies. The directions that some of the fighting styles have taken in their growth have removed some of their bite, though, removing them from the realm of real 'combative' arts. For the best view of the growth and history of martial arts, let us look at the origin and growth of empty hand fighting.

The oldest records we have concerning unarmed combat are hieroglyphics from the Egyptian pyramids, showing Egypt's military men of the Old Kingdom practicing techniques that look like boxing. These are from around 4,000 BC. Other pictures that resemble fighting styles (codified systems of combat) have turned up in the ruins of Sumer in Mesopotamia from about 3,000 BC and in Bein Hasan in Egypt from about 2,300 BC.

It is assumed that some of these styles passed over to Greece through the Aegean civilizations. A fresco has been found on Thera, a small volcanic island midway between Turkey and Greece, that shows two youths with what appears to be leather gloves on their right hands engaged in boxing. This has been dated to around 1,520 BC. From there we move to Greece herself where, in 648 BC, a fighting style called Pankration was officially adopted into the Olympic Games. Pankration means literally 'a game of all powers' which refers to the use of the entire body as a weapon. Both Homer and Plato have recorded the use of Pankration as rough matches in which the winner was often determined by at least a knockout, but as often by the death of one of the participants. Tales abound of the prowess of Greek boxers. Greugas and Damoxenus fought a match around 400 BC in which Damoxenus killed Greugas with an open spear hand thrust to the armpit. Theogenes, a champion of the same century, is credited with knocking out 2,102 opponents, of whom 1,800 died as a result.

Though boxing and wrestling were distinct arts, the Greeks combined the two to form Pankration. No such thing as a foul existed. The Greeks eventually abandoned it as too cruel, but during the time of their Empire the Romans revived it for their superbly trained Legion-naires and for gladiatorial contests.

India is the next step on our journey to the East. Temple statues have been found there, dating from around 1,200 to 1,000 BC, show-ing men and gods in various postures that are still used in empty hand combat. It is also recorded that the warrior caste, the Kshatrya, from which Gautama the Buddha came, practiced a form of empty hand fighting called Vajramushti which involved striking certain vital points of the body with specific parts of the hands and feet. The first vital points were reputedly discovered by an Indian prince of the warrior caste by stabbing hundreds of slaves with needles and recording the effects of each stab for reaction. Buddhist documents record specific strategies of Indian empty hand fighting — reverse techniques, ex-change of blows, and combined strikes. Yoga-like exercises were us-ed for stretching and for health by the warrior class also. There is a theory that Pankration was carried to India by Alexander the Great's forces and it then blended with the native fighting art. There are many similarities between Pankration and Vajramushti, enough so that this theory may have some substance.

The oldest records of Japan show a native art dating back to 450 BC as a grappling system. It became the basis for Sumo, modern Japanese wrestling, and was called Kumi Uchi. At that time it was primarily a means of bringing your opponent to the ground and maim-ing or killing him. A special version was taught called O Yorio Kumi Uchi (Grappling in the Great Harness), referring to grappling with an armored opponent when the grappler was also armored.

China had some basic systems of codified empty hand fighting that were still in the developmental stage when the 29th Patriarch of Bud-dhism arrived from India, the monk Bodhidharma. He had travelled alone on foot over land from India to China in approximately 520 AD at the request of Emperor Wu to teach at the Imperial Court. This was no small feat, for the area that he crossed has some of the highest mountains in the world and is still infested with bandits and fierce wild animals.

When Bodhidharma arrived at the Imperial Court, he displeased the Emperor in what has become a famous dialogue between Emperor and monk, and was banished from the court but allowed to wander as he chose in China. He finally settled at a Taoist temple in northern China, sitting facing a wall in meditation for nine years before attempting to teach the monks of the temple what became known as Zen Buddhism (or Chan in China). The temple was the Shaolin. He also taught the monks of the temple the rudiments of an empty hand fighting system that has come to be known as Shaolin Chuan Fa (Shaolin Fist Law or Methods), Shorinji Kenpo (the Japanese reading of the Kanji, the pictographs, for Shaolin Fist Law), and the Ng Ying Ga (the highly stylized Five Animal Form). His original system is still existent in the Ekkin Sutra.

Kenpo gradually travelled to many other countries throughout the Orient through Buddhist missionaries, wars, and contact through trade agreements. Korea and Okinawa in particular were affected by the introduction of codified fighting systems that they blended with their native fighting styles to form whole new branches of the fighting arts. Each style evolved gradually to meet the needs of the local practitioners. For example, in China, the people in the North had plenty of room to move about and their fighting styles made use of high kicks and long range hitting techniques. In the crowded cities of the south where room was at a premium low kicks and close range fighting techniques were more common.

Moving West, we also find other codified empty hand fighting styles. The Norse and Germanics that migrated westward out of the Caucasius Mountain region brought with them a system called Klima, which is called Glimae in Iceland today. One of the off-shoots of that great migration was the conquering of India by the people that came to be the Kshatrya, so that the two arts, Glimae and Vajramushti, are related. The Helenes that settled in Greece were also part of that migration, and they later developed Pankration. Some of the last remnants of this fighting style, that may be the sun source of all empty hand fighting styles, may be found in Iceland and in the Basque Hills of Spain and France today.

As the need for individual combat proficiency was replaced by the formation of armies where individual skills were subordinate to the whole, and weapons of more and more sophistication became available, empty hand fighting skills became less and less valued. Personal warfare became a thing of the past, by and large, or such was the general consensus.

As a result of this trend toward high technology combat, the use of the fists and feet began to devolve from highly refined fighting systems to mere sport for the sake of entertainment. The western arts became boxing and wrestling. While each of these retain traces of their lethal origins, they are not sufficient for use in deadly combat. Also, and perhaps more importantly, none of the sports teach the underlying principles and spirit which is the foundation of the warrior's skill in combat. Participants in sports do not require that kind of motivation. Matches are often reduced to games of tag or the crudest of brawls that not even undisciplined street fighters would engage in. The Eastern martial arts have largely fallen into the same morass. While they maintain a higher degree of combative method in their training, too many masters have allowed their styles to become strictly sport-oriented. Tournaments are fought with no contact rules and too often resemble games of tag. Many traditional techniques that are held dear are no longer appropriate for use in life-or-death encounters. Those times when Eastern martial arts *were* truly life-or-death fighting arts are long passed and their techniques have failed to change with the times.

Virtually every military force in the world teaches some kind of empty hand combat methods, but not to the point where the average soldier is proficient in them. Some elite units are trained in traditional methods that have been stripped down to the essence of 'what works'. This training often deals with how to take a weapon away from an opponent when you are unarmed, and not in overall fighting skills. Soldiers stationed in the Orient are often encouraged to study the local fighting arts, but again we run into the traditional wall. This is how some of the traditional martial arts found their way to the US after WW II — with returning service men. Generally the hand-to-hand that is taught the average soldier is a blend of several martial arts. One such example is judo and boxing which was taught post WW II GI's. Other systems are taken from jujutsu, wrestling, boxing, karate, fencing, and other traditional arts, all blended together to form what is hoped to be a combat-efficient method of fighting if unarmed.

Paramilitary and police forces are also trained in the rudiments of empty hand self-defense, but rarely are they taught enough to really protect themselves and have come to rely on chemical or electrical weapons when non-lethal force is called for to subdue a miscreant. A trained fighter, particularly one that has been trained in the combative aspects of a martial art, can often overcome an armed opponent if the martial artist sees the opponent reach for the weapons or if the opponent allows his concentration to lapse for a moment when confronting the martial artist. Reliance on weapons in close combat is not good. It creates a weakness in one's skills.

There are practical alternatives to spending at least ten years of your life in mastering a traditional art, then straining the unnecessary from it. There are a multitude of 'eclectic' fighting styles that teach pure fighting, but many of them are dedicated to either kick-boxing or tournament play and not fighting for your life in self-defense. By taking what works the best from various traditional styles and blending them together into one practical fighting system, as well as the specified training methods for each individual area (i.e. blocks, kicks, footwork, etc.), and then combining the individual skills into one spontaneous whole, one may get the very best from the most fighting styles, boiled down to the basics of practical combat.

This is what is attempted here. Unfortunately, there is no secret pill one may take to become a proficient fighter. It takes long hours of work and sweat to become proficient at anything; fighting is no exception, primarily because no two encounters are the same. In your training you must first master the basics of each technique, then combine them, still using the proper body mechanics, and in the end be able to come up with the correct move without having to think about what to do. While this is intended as a nuts-and-bolts manual for training in combative martial arts, both in the relevant mental and physical aspects, it takes time to learn the skills and more time to internalize them so that you can act spontaneously. The final process is to transfer these actions and lessons to everyday life making yourself one with your way.

Chapter Two

Health

Health to a warrior is as much physical as it is mental. To be effective as a fighter and creative and dynamic as a person, you must have both a healthy mind and body. One without the other leads to lethargy, which, in combat or any stress situation can get you killed. If you are not fit you will always follow the easiest course of action which often leads to entrapment or defeat. If you are not confident in your technique or training, you may hesitate at a time when action is the key to victory.

Breathing

The practice of any combative art places special emphasis on breathing and endurance. Boxers call it 'wind' and attribute good wind to strenuous training. Training is indeed the key to endurance but not necessarily in the sense boxers refer to training. Correct breathing methods are more essential to development of the mind-body form of health sought for combative training than is mere physical conditioning.

It is essential to healthy life no matter what occupation you are engaged in to breathe well and fully. Fresh air restores energy that is depleted in strenuous activity; it circulates nutrients in the blood; and it allows one to remain strong and resilient. Improper breathing, shallow breathing that does not fully aerate the lungs, actually hampers restoration of the body and causes mental as well as physical fatigue. In order to maintain a condition of top responsiveness both physically and mentally, one must learn to overcome their natural breathing 'habit' and learn to use new ones. Natural in this case is used to describe an acquired habit. Natural breathing is what is about to be described but is programmed out of us as we grow from infancy. Animals and infants breathe this way naturally but people, as they grow older, develop tensions of which they are often unaware in response to stress in their lives. The muscular effects of these tensions center in the solar plexus, making the diaphragm tense and breathing shallow.

Physically the mechanical aspect of breathing manifests itself through elastic movement of the lungs, and the activity of the thoracic cavity where the lungs are contained. The twelve ribs on each side of this cavity have a number of different muscles between each one. The main muscle involved is the diaphragm, which separates the chest cavity from the abdominal cavity. During exhalation it compresses the lungs, during inhalation it expands with the lungs. The nervous system is under direct control of the breath. It is divided into two parts, the cerebro-spinal and the autonomic systems. The cerebro-spinal consists of the brain and spinal cord, along with the nerves that branch off of it. The autonomic is that part located in the thoracic, abdominal, and pelvic cavities. Its function is the regulation of all organ and glandular activity and consists of a double chain of 'ganglia' located on each side of the spinal cord. Ganglia are a collection of nerve bodies, with fibers branching out to all the organs of the body. At various points they intertwine to form nerve plexus. From this you can see that breathing is a function that reaches throughout your entire body.

The proper method of breathing that makes the most efficient use of our own body is to breathe deeply and slowly. Use the nose and not the mouth to inhale. In the following exercise keep these two points in mind: (1) breathe in deeply using the diaphragm and not the upper chest, and (2) exhale the air from the lower stomach-diaphragm up, not from the chest down.

Begin by standing with your feet parallel, about shoulder width apart, with the hands hanging relaxed at your sides. Keep your back and head straight, erect, but relax your entire body, not tensing anything. It is helpful to calm your mind also, to quiet the mental chatter so that your mind is focused on your breathing only and not on anything else. Forcefully exhale all of the breath from your body from the diaphragm up, through your nostrils. Push the air out of your lower abdomen by contracting the muscles of the stomach-diaphragm slowly. As soon as you have completely exhaled, start inhaling slowly through the nostrils letting it fill your body from the lower abdomen upward by relaxing the tensed muscles slowly. Hold the air in your lungs for a slow count of ten at first. Every time you perform the exercise try to hold the air in longer. Repeat this cycle for five minutes. This breathing method helps to reduce stress and helps you to relax and concentrate. When you first arise in the morning or at any time during the day when you need to relax or feel distracted by weariness or tension, perform this exercise. In the heat of combat, if you train in this breathing method, you should fall into the rhythmic deep breathing naturally.

For empty hand fighting, use of this exercise helps train one in the proper method by repetition. This next exercise is movement with breathing to explain how it benefits one in combat. From the Ready stance, as you inhale and hold your breath for a slow count of ten, step one foot forward. As it is placed on the floor exhale strongly. Inhale again and hold the breath, step the other foot forward and exhale strongly as it hits the floor. In practical use this simulates the expulsion of breath as you execute any given technique. You exhale when you exert your muscles and inhale when you are at rest. There is more detailed instruction of this method in the technique section. The effects of this form of breathing are numerous. The psychological benefits are greater power of concentration, feeling more at ease at all times and not tense. It strengthens the will and begins to coordinate the mind and the body. This is essential for combat. Physically, deep breathing more fully oxygenates the lungs and blood stream, generally giving one better respiration. Shallow breathing usually does not aerate the bottom one-third of the lungs which is where many lung diseases begin. This method reaches the entire volume of the lungs, increasing the lungs' capacity to hold air.

Concentration

Fighting is something that holds you to the present, to the moment, like few other activities can. One lapse of your attention, by external or internal distractions, can be painful at the least, fatal at most. Thus you must cultivate concentration, but not to the point of 'tunnel vision'. That total concentration on one thing is fine for sport-oriented fighters, but in combat you must not let what is in front of you distract you from what may be flanking you or sneaking up from behind. To keep this concentration, indeed to find it in the first place, one must remain calm mentally. If your thoughts are whirling through your mind you will not be able to act without conscious effort in a fight, nor will you be able to deal with multiple opponents at once. For example, if you are confronted by an aggressive opponent and you are so preoccupied with him that you fail to hear his partner sneaking up on you, you may lose.

Training for proper breathing is one way to learn this concentration. Meditation is another way. For a warrior's purpose meditation may be done in the standing position with the body relaxed and the feet spread shoulder width apart, hands hanging loosely at the sides. Begin the deep breathing exercise. Every time you exhale count backward from one hundred, one number at a time, until you have reached zero. Keep the torso erect, head straight, and the body relaxed. You must keep your mind focused on your breathing, which teaches the mind to be silent, not to wander off on unbidden tangents. If you lose the count, stop and start at one hundred again. You may choose certain subjects to meditate on such as honor, courage, technique, or you may simply meditate on concentration and breathing. When you have reached zero in your countdown you should have attained the Alpha state, similar to when you are asleep, where your mind is emitting Alpha waves. The mind is silent and you are in a state of total concentration. The goal of the warrior is to achieve this state without conscious meditation during combat, so that your mind and body are free to flow by themselves, guided subconsciously by your training. In this state you react to your opponent subconsciously, with no intellectualization of his movements or yours, just reaction.

Training the Body

It is best to train the body with the idea of quality over quantity exercises. Cheating on any exercise, doing it in such a way that you do not obtain the greatest benefit from it but so that it is easier for you, robs you of your own time. Performing any exercise correctly, even if slowly, with concentration on the purpose of the movements will insure that you get the full benefit of your training. It will also strengthen the tendons and harden the muscles as well as build greater physical endurance. Use the proper breathing method when performing any exercise.

Recommended exercises are listed in separate sections with brief descriptions of the areas of the body that each exercise works and the benefit of each exercise to a warrior. You may choose any of the exercises, mixing the calisthenics with the weight training if you wish, but it is recommended that you do some of them daily. A little work every day is much better than going ''whole hog'' only for a few days. A minimum would be every other day for a serious workout. Regularity is the key.

Equipment

For stretching and calisthenics there is nothing essential. A dip rack for the dips, a broom stick for the trunk twisters and a kitchen chair for the rising kicks would be helpful. The dips can be done in another form where all you need is something to brace your hands on behind you, such as a chair. Trunk twisters can be done with the arms extended without a broom stick. A wall or nearby tree can serve as a brace for rising kicks.

The conditioning may be enhanced with a heavy canvas or leather punching bag such as boxers use and the nearby availability of a tree. A hard rubber pad is also needed, and a piece of pipe approximately two inches in diameter.

The weight training requires weights, bars and benches. You can go to a gymnasium and find all of the equipment you need, and more. Or, if you have the funds and the room, you can purchase everything that you need for home use. All you need basically is a bar, two hundred pounds of weights, and a bench which can be bought or made.

The stretching and weight training should be done, for the sake of safety, with a partner. There are several stretching devices that are very helpful. The most prominent is a rope and pulley arrangement that allows you to stretch yourself by attaching your foot to one end of a rope which runs upward to a pulley and then downward into your hands. Another is called the Rack, a recent invention with a crank handle that you control, which stretches you with each crank of the handle. There are several models of these on the market.

Caution: Before beginning this series of exercises, first consult your physician. Explain to him that you are going to train in martial arts and describe the type of exercise program. Be sure that you are in good enough health to undertake this program!

Also, do not force yourself when you are tired or sore, to continue to the point where you injure yourself. This is especially true for weight training and for stretching where you can easily tear muscles. You will get sore, but that will work out eventually. Serious injuries will stop you from further training and impair your health later, while these exercises, if done in moderation, will improve your overall health and increase your power for self-defense.

Stretching

This is something that cannot be overemphasized. Stretching is beneficial to everyone, not just a warrior, but for anyone that wishes to enjoy more flexibility and agility. Keeping the joints loose and the body limber will ensure better health in future years and much more comfortable body movements now. For the warrior, however, being able to move fluidly and keeping that flexibility is vital. Stretching may be done both before and after training: before a session to limber up so that none of the muscles are damaged because they are cold and stiff; after training to warm down so the muscles do not get stiff and sore when they no longer are in use in such drastic fashion.

Caution: Again, you are cautioned not to force your stretching.

A. Forward bends — Stand with your feet together and your arms crossed over your chest. Lean forward at the waist allowing your knees to bend slightly. Let your crossed elbows and your head fall forward, trying to reach the ground with them. Do not force the downward motion. Relax the muscles and let gravity pull you down. Repeat this ten times holding the downward portion of the movement for a brief count before straightening up. Do ten more repetitions staying bent over, holding the elbows at the low point of the stretch, and straighten your knees. Hold that position for several seconds.

B. Front rising kicks — Assume a right Front stance (see stance section) with the hands in the mid-level guard. Swing the left leg, knee locked straight, forward and up pulling the left hand to the rear as you kick the leg up. Try to get the foot higher with each repetition. Perform ten on the left leg, then change into a left Front stance and perform ten kicks with the right leg.

C. Side rising kicks — Assume a Straddle stance and face to the left. Step the right foot behind the left foot then swing the left foot up and to the left side. Keep the knee locked when doing this. Pull your left arm behind you when you kick. Perform ten of these on the left side, turn and face to the right, then perform ten of these on the right side.

D. Partner assisted front stretch — Stand in a Ready stance with your partner facing you kneeling. Place your right foot on his left shoulder and bend the knee of the left leg. Keeping the knee of your right leg straight, have him slowly stand up straight. If his shoulder height is not enough to give you a full stretch, have him push your leg up higher with his hands. At first, you may want to do this with something behind you to lean on for support. One of these on each leg is sufficient.

E. Partner assisted side stretch — Assume a Straddle stance facing to the left and have your training partner kneel on your left side facing you. Place your left foot on his right shoulder with the toes pointing to his left, bending the knee of the right leg. Have him stand up slowly keeping the knee of the left leg locked straight, pushing upward with his hands if his shoulder height is not enough. One of these on each leg is sufficient.

F. Partner assisted round stretch — This is the same as the partner assisted front stretch, but your partner holds your foot turned into the position that it assumes for a round kick. (See kick section.) The foot is turned to the side. For example, the left foot is turned to the right and the right foot is turned to the left. One on each leg is sufficient.

G. Front splits — Stand in a Ready stance. Slide your right leg forward keeping it straight, while your left leg bends from its stationary position. Slide the left leg straight back. Turn the instep of the left foot to the floor and the heel of the right foot to the floor, raising the toes of the right foot up. Place both hands palm down on the floor on each side of you for support, and lower yourself as far as you can into the split. When you get as far down as you can, relax all of the muscles that are tense from the strain and hold that position for a brief count. Return to the Ready stance and repeat the process by sliding the left leg forward and the right leg backward this time. One on each side is sufficient.

H. Side splits — Stand in a Ready stance and slide your right foot to the right. Lower your hands to touch the floor in front of you for support and lower yourself into a side split by extending both legs out to the sides as far as they can go. When you have reached the lowest point of your stretch that you can handle, lean forward and touch your nose to the floor. Do this ten times then return to the Ready stance. One side split is sufficient.

I. Sitting splits — Sit on the ground and pull your heels up close to your buttocks with the soles touching each other. Hold the toes with both hands and apply downward pressure with the elbows to the knees, pushing them as close to the floor as you can. Have your training partner either stand on both of your knees, pushing them downward, or lean on them from the front with both palms. One of these is sufficient. They stretch the hips for greater range of movement and are essential to your stretching.

J. Two legged front stretch — Sit with your legs together, knees bent slightly. Bend forward at the waist and grab the bottom of your feet with both hands. Pull your forehead forward to touch your knees, then slowly straighten your knees. Repeat this several times, exhaling as you straighten your knees.

K. Alternate leg stretch — From a squatting position extend the left leg to the left side, toes pointing upward, knee locked straight. Keeping your knee straight, lower yourself until you feel tension in the extended leg. Shift your weight until the other leg is extended and straight, and your weight is on the left leg which is now bent. Repeat this ten times on each leg.

L. Hand bridge — From a prone position on your back, bend your knees and pull your heels close to your buttocks. Place your hands, palms down on the floor with the fingers turned in to your shoulders. Slowly push yourself upward until you are in a full upward bow, then lower yourself to the floor repeating this ten times.

M. The combination stretch — Stand in a Ready stance and lean forward with the knees bent and the arms crossed over the chest. Let your head fall forward with the elbows reaching the floor. Slowly straighten the knees and hold that position for a brief count. Place your palms on the floor, then reach back and grasp the calves with both hands. Bend your knees again and pull your forehead to your shins, then slowly straighten the knees and hold this stretch. Return your palms to the floor and walk them forward about three feet in front of you. Lower your chest to the ground and slide forward letting your belly drag on the ground. Push your chest upward and arch your back. Reverse this movement until you are arched upward again, then walk your hands backward to your feet, palms still flat on the floor. Straighten up into the Ready stance. Raise your hands over your head and stretch backward trying to touch your hands to the floor behind you. Repeat the series five times.

Training requirements: To maintain flexibility after you have begun stretching exercises they must be performed every day, though not the entire routine. Try to find some time during the day when you can perform at least the stretches you have found the most rewarding, that work the 'problem areas' most of us have. As your flexibility increases repeat each exercise, even those listed as one being sufficient; the more repetitions the better. The more you do, the greater the endurance in your lower body and the easier you will be able to move in combat if you ever have to.

Calisthenics

A. Five sets of ten dips — By doing these in a rack consisting of two parallel bars about four and a half feet off the ground you work the triceps and the upper chest muscles, adding power to cross body technique. There is another way to perform dips if no rack is available. Find a bench, a low wall or chair, anything you can lay your palms on top of which is about as high, and place your palms on top of it, face down, fingers pointing in toward your body. Kick your feet forward so that the entire weight of your body is supported by your palms. Lower yourself by bending your arms to the floor or as close as you can go depending on the height of the object you are leaning on. Hold the lowered position for a second then push yourself up to the raised position. Add more repetitions to each set as you are able.

B. Five sets of ten handstand push-ups — Perform a handstand in front of a wall and allow your feet to fall backward to touch the wall for support. (Your back should be to the wall.) Lower yourself as close to the floor as you are able, then straighten your arms and push yourself back up. It may take a while to build up to five sets of ten so do as many as you can per set. These build the upper chest, shoulders, and triceps for powerful straight or upward techniques. When you are able to perform five sets of ten, try doing them without letting your feet touch the wall.

C. At least fifty regular push-ups — Done on the palms of the hands and the balls of the feet these work the triceps, biceps, shoulders, and chest for thrusting power. Do as many as you can in one set and go on. There are variations of these in the hand conditioning section.

D. Five sets of twenty trunk twisters — These toughen the ribs with ridges of muscle and provide more power for hip actions which predicate all technique. If there is a broomstick available, or any straight stick of equal length, put it behind your head and drape your hands over it at arm's length. Pivot as far as possible from the hips to each side in wide semi-circles, keeping your back straight and your upper body relaxed. Do not tense your head, neck, or shoulders as you can easily pull a muscle. If no stick is available, extend the arms out straight to each side and perform the exercise. As your endurance builds, add more repetitions to each set.

E. Five sets of ten diagonal toe touches — These also build the muscle tone in the frontal abdomen and strengthen hip rotation in techniques. They work to stretch the rear thigh muscles as well, for greater flexibility. Place the feet shoulder width apart in the Ready stance (see stance section) with the hands on the hips. Bend forward touching the toes of the right foot with the fingers of the left hand, return to the Ready stance and repeat by touching the toes of the left foot with the fingers of the right hand. This series counts as one repetition. After you become more flexible, close the hands into fists and touch the toes with the knuckles. Later reach for the outside of the foot with the fingertips. Finally, place the palm of each hand on the outside of the foot when you perform the repetitions. As they become easier add more repetitions to each set.

F. Fifty bent-legged sit-ups — These may be performed in sets of varying numbers or a single set. They tighten the upper stomach muscles and abdomen which aid in kicking as well as buffering the force of incoming mid-level blows. Doing them bent-legged provides a greater degree of tension on the muscles involved, hardening them faster. Begin by lying flat on your back with your hands clasped across your stomach. Pull your heels in close to your buttocks, keeping your bent knees together and sit up as far as you can. Exhale as you sit up, inhale as you lower yourself to the prone position. Each sit-up is one repetition. As you are able, add at least one repetition per day per workout.

G. Fifty side sit-ups — These are similar to the above, but they work the abdominal oblique muscles. Lay flat on your back, relaxed, with your hands at your sides. Cross your left leg over your right leg at the knees and place the left foot flat on the floor. Raise the right leg six inches off the floor and hold it there. Keeping tension on the stomach muscles, raise your torso off the floor ten to twelve inches, twisting to your left as you raise yourself. Relax and return to the floor. Each one of these counts as one repetition. After you have perform-ed fifty on the left side, reverse the position and perform fifty on the right side. These are to be done in conjunction with bent-legged sit-ups, not as a replacement.

H. Run in place — Do this with high knee pull, working the hips and stretching the thighs as you perform the exercise. This will also increase your endurance. Pull the knee as high toward the chest as you can, and maintain proper breathing. Run in place for at least twelve minutes, then add more time as you can, increasing your speed, too.

I. Two sets of fifty deep knee bends — These work the thigh muscles for more power in the legs, enhancing all your movements and kicks. Assume a Ready stance with your hands at your sides. Bend the knees until your thighs are parallel to the floor and extend your arms straight out in front of you. Keep both feet flat on the floor. As you straighten the knees, bend forward and place the palms of both hands on the floor until the knees are straight, stretching the rear thigh muscles. Straighten up and resume the Ready stance. Each one of these counts as one repetition. As you can, increase the number of repetitions per set.

J. Five sets of one-legged deep knee bends — Begin in the Ready stance. Bend the knee of one leg and bring it up behind you so that you can grab the ankle with your other hand. Bend the knee of the other leg and lower yourself until your supporting leg thigh is parallel to the floor. Inhale as you do this, then exhale as you straighten the supporting leg and resume a Ready stance still holding the bent leg. Keep your back straight and extend the free arm out in front of you to help maintain your balance. When you can do five sets of ten, add more repetitions per set on each leg.

K. Five sets of ten neck bridges — This builds up a strong but flexible neck and is used by every athlete that ever has strain placed on his neck. Begin by lying prone on the floor with your hands palm down on the floor beside you. Bend your legs and tuck your feet up as close to your buttocks as you can. Using your neck, arch your back and bring your shoulders off the floor so that your weight rests on the top of your head, supported by your neck. Hold this for several seconds then return to the prone. Do not use your hands in any way.

Leave them on the floor. When you can do five sets of ten, add more repetitions to each set.

There are further specialized calisthenics in the kicking section.

Weight Resistance Training

It is a common misconception that weight training stiffens the body or adds too much bulk. It can happen, but if you work with the idea of repetitions and muscular definition in mind rather than sheer power for one lift, you will be all right. Many athletes use weight training to aid their overall training, including fighters and soldiers. Strength is a definite plus in combat. Weight training shows the fastest results of any training program. Increase weight only in small increments as you build strength, and never lift without a workout partner or spotter.

A. Five sets of ten bench presses — These firm the chest and increase straight line power. For the warrior the grip should be held at shoulder width on the bar. When you bring the bar down to the chest do not bounce it; rather, stop it and let it rest there for a second before pushing it up to full extension of the arms. Inhale as you lower the weight and exhale as you push it up.

B. Five sets of ten incline presses — These build the upper torso muscles adding power to the shoulders and chest. An incline bench is needed for this exercise. The handstand push-up works the same area of the body. Perform these with a shoulder width grip, inhaling as you lower the bar to your chest, exhaling as you press the bar up. Pause with the bar on your chest for a second.

C. Five sets of ten military presses — These strengthen the shoulders, neck, and upper back muscles, as well as the triceps and lattissimus muscles. They add power for downward strikes and grappling situations, and for pulling. Use a shoulder width grip, inhale as you lower the bar to your shoulders, exhale as you press the bar upward. *Do not* thrust upward with the legs or jerk the weight up. Keep your neck relaxed.

D. Five sets of ten standing curls — These build the biceps for added power in pulling and grappling techniques, as well as strengthening the elbows so that they are less easily damaged. Hold the bar slightly closer than shoulder width and exhale as you pull the bar upward to your chest. Do this slowly. Do not rock at the hips or lean backward at the waist. Inhale as you lower the bar slowly from the chest to the lower abdomen. Straighten the arms at extension and pause for a moment before you bring the arms upward again.

E. Five sets of ten preacher bench curls — The preacher bench is a slanted rest for the arms. You sit behind it and pull (curl) the bar to you with your elbows resting on the slanted portion of the bench. This does the same thing that the standing curl does but provides more strain and concentration; thus it does not replace the standing curl, but supplements it and should be done during the same workout.

F. Five sets of ten prone dumbbell cross arm extensions — These are done lying flat on your back on a bench with one arm holding the dumbbell and extended straight up in the air. The other is crossed over the chest and supports the extended arm at the bicep just above the elbow. Lower the extended arm across the chest, only bend it at the elbow, and bring the dumbbell to the opposite shoulder inhaling as you do so. Exhale and straighten the arm without using the shoulder to raise it. This works the triceps and increases across the body striking power.

G. Five sets of ten standing French curls — These may be done standing or seated as they primarily work the tricep. This increases the downward strikes. Grasp the bar slightly closer than shoulder width and raise it over your head, palms upward and knuckles to the rear. Inhaling, lower the bar slowly to your neck by bending the elbows. Keep the elbows as close together as you can. Exhale, and raise the bar over your head again. Do not use the hips to throw the bar up, or jerk it upward with your shoulders. Pause for a moment both when you lower it to the back of your neck and when you raise it to full extension.

H. Five sets of ten pullovers — These may be done with either a bar or dumbbell. Lay prone on your back on a bench with the weight on your chest. If done with a dumbbell, clasp it with both hands by the web between thumb and forefingers; if done with a bar, grasp it at shoulder width or closer. Lower your head over the end of the bench so that your shoulders are on the very edge. Slowly, keeping your back flat and not arching it, lift the weight off your chest and lower it past your face to the ground. (Bend your arms with the bar; with the dumbbell keep both arms straight.) Pause for a moment and pull the weight back up to your chest, exhaling. This exercise armor-plates the ribs and adds tremendous power to downward strikes.

I. Five sets of ten wrist curls — This is done seated. Grasp the bar at shoulder width, palms turned up, and place your forearms on your knees so that the hands hang over the knee caps. Lower the bar by bending the wrists until they touch the knees, inhaling. Curl the wrists upward as far as they will go, exhaling. Keep both feet flat on the floor. This builds the forearms for striking, blocking, and adds strength to the grip. The variation of this is to turn the palms down when you grab the bar and curl the wrists backward as far as they will go, then lower them to touch the knee. This is called the reverse wrist curl and may be done in conjunction with the regular wrist curl.

J. Five sets of ten lattissimus pulls — These are done by digging one end of a weight bar in the ground, putting weight on the other end, straddling it and grasping it just below the weight plates, then pulling it upward to your chest. You must hunch over slightly to do this. Do not sway up and down. This works the lattissimus muscles, contributing to strong elbow strikes and downward techniques as well as firming the muscles along the ribs from armpit to hip.

K. Five sets of ten deadlifts — Using the weight for more repetitions can harden the muscles of the lower back, protecting your kidneys as well as providing you with much greater power in lifting or grappling situations. Grasp the bar with the left hand turned inward and the right hand turned outward (or the reverse), bend your legs, push with the legs and straighten your back lifting the weight. Inhale as you lower the bar to the ground and exhale as you lift the bar.

L. Five sets of ten squats — Combine this exercise with plenty of stretching because squats tend to tighten the leg muscles. Squats strengthen thighs and hips for more fluid movement and powerful kicks or throwing actions. Take the bar on the shoulders behind your head, with your hands gripping the bar slightly wider than your shoulder width. Bend the knees until the thighs are parallel with the floor, inhaling as you do so. Then straighten the knees, thrusting upward with the thighs, exhaling.

Conditioning

Body conditioning in the fighting arts is more specialized than in any other sport or physical activity. It is the toughening of specific areas of the body that make contact in strikes or blocks to withstand the tremendous impact of properly delivered techniques. Deforming parts of the body is not part of conditioning however, and anyone that advocates or participates in such actions is not very bright. Conditioning does eventually toughen by building callouses and deadening or desensitizing certain areas. No injury is sustained, and it is a gradual process requiring time and dedication to make it effective. It is not essential to your fighting ability however, and is considered optional.

The methods of conditioning listed here may be done without supervision and without any exotic solutions to soak the areas that you have been conditioning. Do not attempt to put full power into your technique in conditioning training at the beginning; it is a gradual process. If you injure your hand from too zealous a beginning you will be unable to pursue further training until the hand is healed, wasting your own time.

A. Foreknuckle push-ups — This is a good starting method for conditioning the fist for striking, and it is the least painful. From the Ready stance, assume the push-up position with your hands clenched tightly into fists. Rest the weight of the upper body on the two fore-knuckles with the fists turned vertically (palms inward, top of the fist pointing straight ahead, in the same method as the punch itself), and the weight of the lower body supported by the balls of the feet. Per-form as many of these as you can in this manner, keeping the wrist firm so that it does not bend. Fifty is a recommended minimum to be done in conjunction with regular push-ups.

B. Heavy bag punching — Without the handwraps and the leather gloves usually used for punching bag training, assume a Fighting stance in front of a heavy bag and perform at least fifty of each punch listed in this manual on each hand. Vary the lead side so that you are used to punching with power with either leg forward. Be sure that you strike the bag solidly, as a grazing blow will rip the knuckles. Use proper tension, exhale at impact, lock the wrist and leave the fist in the bag. In a normal strike in combat you would withdraw the fist im-mediately, but for conditioning let the bag rebound from your fist. This method is used for all blows, not just punching.

C. Sandbag punching — The bag may be made of vinyl, burlap, or cotton, and filled with either fine sand or beans. Either lay it on a firm flat surface or hang it on a wall. Perform fifty of each strike and thrust of the system on it, using the same rules as for heavy bag punching. When you have attained some success with your condi-tioning, fill the bag with fine sand which is denser, providing more resistance.

D. Fingertip push-ups — Assume the push-up position with all of your upper body weight supported on the tips of your fingers, which should be spread out at first. As your fingers get stronger, bring them in closer together until you have them touching each other at the tips. This strengthens the grip and the fingers for the fingertip thrust. These are also done in conjunction with other push-ups, not replacing them. A recommended minimum would be fifty.

E. Bean bag exercise — Assume a front Straddle stance. With the bean bag in your left hand, toss it in the air to your center line. Grab it with your right hand, digging the fingers into it as you catch it. Toss it in the air with the right hand and catch it with the left hand. Do this until you are worn out. When the beans become too light, replace them with steel ball bearings. This strengthens the grip and shoulders.

F. Thrusting bucket — Fill a regular bucket with beans and stand over it in a front Straddle stance. Perform alternating fingertip thrusts into it, trying to penetrate to the bottom of the bucket. When you no longer feel much resistance from the beans, exchange them for fine sand.

G. Bear claw — Use a hard rubber pad approximately two inches thick. Place it on a concrete block and kneel in front of it. Make a claw hand and strike the pad with a snapping motion of the hand and wrist. Drive into the pad and do not let your hand bounce off of it. Alternate hands, performing at least fifty strikes with each hand.

H. Sword Hand — Strike a heavy bag fifty times with each method of using the Sword Hand. Use each hand.

I. Three hundred strikes — Use a two-inch or larger diameter pipe, and strike it three hundred times with the sword edge of each hand in a downward striking method. Do not let the hand bounce off of the pipe. This is the best way to condition the sword edge of the hand.

J. Tree strikes — Stand in front of a tree with rough bark in a Fighting or Straddle stance and deliver palm strikes to the tree with alternate hands. Perform at least fifty strikes with each hand. Aside from toughening the palms, this builds strong thrusts.

K. Forearms — The forearm is used extensively in blocking and many of the blocks are strikes in themselves. Therefore, the forearms should be conditioned to take and deliver strong blows. It is possible to condition your forearms so that you can block and deflect blows from wooden batons without pain, though that takes a while. The first exercise is striking the forearms on a rounded object; the two inch pipe used for Sword Hand conditioning, for example. Use the meaty inner and outer portions of the forearm, not letting it bounce off of the pipe. Start with fifty repetitions on each arm and work up to three hundred.

The second method requires a partner. Stand facing each other in Ready stances, and, with opposite arms, strike the forearms together. Obtain a rhythm alternating the arms, going from mid to low level and then high level so that all blocking surfaces of the forearm are equally conditioned. You may perform this for a specified period of time or for three hundred repetitions.

L. Foot conditioning — Since the average practitioner of combative martial arts will not be fighting barefoot, the amount of emphasis on foot conditioning is less than for the hands. If you want to condition the feet, kick the heavy bag with the appropriate part of the foot fifty times with each leg, for each kick in the system. Tree kicking is also recommended.

M. Shin conditioning — Many of your kicks will be blocked in your shin area, which is also the target for many low level kicks. The shins, like the forearms, should be conditioned to accept some punishment. Kick a heavy bag, using the front of the shin as a striking area, and do not let the shin bounce off of the bag. Begin with twenty repetitions on each leg and work up to three hundred.

Another method is to use a rolling pin and roll it up and down your shin one hundred times on each shin. At first do not apply much pressure, gradually increasing it.

N. Elbows — Strike the heavy bag with fifty of each strike in the system on each arm. Striking the bean bag is also recommended.

O. Knees — Strike the heavy bag with fifty of each knee kick on each leg.

Practicing all of the strikes and kicks in the system on the heavy bag without protection gear will build strong and accurate technique, and will harden the striking surfaces at the same time. Apply full force to the strikes only after you have worked on conditioning for at least three months, then try to strike through the bag with each blow.

Chapter Three

Traditions

True traditions are not made arbitrarily by men; they develop from a social desire to adopt certain concepts and methods of doing things. They grow and expand as men do, and they must never freeze into rigid molds which will suffocate the people bound by them. They should be flexible and change with the times, allowing those who live by them to grow spiritually within their framework, stimulating new responses which in turn become part of the tradition. Often, when certain traditions are formed, the period is only a phase that in itself is in a process of evolution; thus, if the traditions formulated during such times are taken too seriously the people will not attempt to evolve or gain new knowledge from sources outside their closed 'traditional' community. This is why the traditional martial arts are being blended with modern fighting requirements and methods to form combat effective fighting systems for self-defense in a modern way.

This section deals briefly with what may become traditions for a modern martial style. It does not hold with the traditional martial arts of the Orient in many ways, yet it uses what is best of them as well as the best of other methods and training procedures. Knowledge, whether traditional or acquired from practical experience, must never be blind.

Clothing

For centuries the Oriental martial artists wore what for them was every day clothing for their particular area. This only made sense to them, since to train in a suit of clothing that they very probably would not be wearing when it came time to fight was foolish. It was many years later that uniforms for training were worn. In Japan the change came when the Samurai class was abolished and men of all stations in life sought training in the martial arts. A 'classless' uniform was required. Similarly, as men of all beliefs and vocations seek the warrior path today, the uniforms of the training hall may vary from the traditional Oriental GI.

The primary demands of clothing for training are that they be durable and allow free movement. Since this training is very active, with some of it conducted out-of-doors, clothing must be comfortable and also give basic protection from the elements. It may be impractical and impossible to train in one's daily clothing. A compromise of sorts must be effected.

Military fatigues are the most durable, comfortable, and loose-fitting that are easily available, other than various martial art uniforms. They can be bought from military surplus dealers at reasonable prices in olive drab (OD) green, or in a variety of camouflage. They can also be found new from many paramilitary supply sources.

Warm up suits and sweat suits will do until you attempt grappling training, at which time your sweat shirts will stretch and tear badly. If military fatigues are worn the sleeves should be rolled down and buttoned at the cuff. Short sleeve shirts should not be worn. Jeans are fine if they do not restrict your movement too much, as are thick denim shirts. You may choose to wear a traditional martial art uniform if you have one already; it is not essential that you wear something other than a traditional GI.

Footwear

Footwear is the most vital aspect of one's training gear. It should, like the clothing, be appropriate to the situation. For martial arts practice with a partner (or a class) a soft-soled shoe or boot is required. There are many canvas or rubber-soled shoes and boots available. There are even shoes specifically designed for martial artists with soft rubber soles much like a tennis shoe in style. Ankle high shoes or boots support the ankle better than do low cuts, and for outdoor training they are generally more protective of the foot. Whatever style of shoe you choose they should be comfortable and fit well, as well as being well cared for. Slip-on shoes should be avoided; lace up styles are better for training. They will not come loose and fly off or be pulled off in a grappling situation.

Paraphernalia

Watches, rings, neck chains, or anything bright or noisy should not be worn during training. Jewelry might injure your training partner or you. Rings may become hung up in clothing or something more substantial, peeling your finger off. Chains can be used to choke you. Watches, rings and large belt buckles may injure your partner. Bright, flashy jewelry or other objects serve to attract attention on the street and may even get in your way in many situations. In combat they might reflect the sun and give your position away to the enemy. All of these things are potential obstacles in the training hall.

Wrist bands are, on the other hand, a different matter. Sturdy leather bands may save your wrist from a knife stroke in self-defense.

They also may serve as a convenient stash for small items that you wish to keep near at hand. The cloth athletic versions absorb moisture and may help you keep a grip on your equipment in combat or self-defense. They should be a dark color. These are strictly for combat-defense situations and are not something that you should wear in the training hall. It is also up to the individual whether or not to wear them.

In self-defense a set of sturdy rings on each hand will act to reinforce the punch, much like a set of 'brass knuckles'. A spiked wrist band will also seriously discourage an opponent from reaching out and grabbing your hand or wrist; if worn on the wrist that is armed, it would be hard for the opponent to control the armed hand. These are 'tricks' however, and should not be relied upon to replace good, solid technique. They are not recommended.

All of your training gear should be kept clean and in good repair. Your fingernails should be kept short so that you do not scratch your partner. Keeping your training equipment in good repair is a sign of the respect that you show for your Way and for yourself.

Ranking

In the traditional schools of martial art there were no systems of ranking such as exist today. One trained until he had mastered the style of his teacher, whether in one year or ten, and received only a certificate to show that he *had* mastered the style. Of course, the student also had the ability to prove mastery as well as the certificate should he be challenged. After receiving said certificate the student often left the master to test his technique in actual battle in wars or duels. In Korea and China a final test was given, often placing the student in danger of serious injury or even death should he fail. It only approximated the fate he would meet in real life, the world outside their temples, should his training not be sufficient. If he passed this test by surviving, he was free to wander outside the temple. Part of the test, usually the final phase, was to move an urn that branded certain marks on his forearms when he moved it, showing his mastery of their Way.

Much later, in Japan, the present system of colored belts was developed. This often gives a false sense of confidence to the holders of certain ranks in the traditional martial arts. A black belt should be able to defend himself against most street assailants, in theory. In practice this is not always the case. On Okinawa, where Karate really developed, the student began with a white belt which, with age and training, became stained brown and then black. Eventually it became worn and threadbare, exposing the white threads again. That was their cycle of ranking and it came about naturally. When you saw a man with a threadbare black and white belt you knew you saw a veteran martial artist, very probably a master or senior student.

What is proposed for ranking in this combative martial style is a headband. It would serve several purposes. It would keep sweat out of the student's eyes; it would help restrain the hair; and it would denote rank in the same manner that the Okinawan white belt did. With long training and sweat it would slowly turn from a light color to a darker one, and then begin to fade out. However, a headband must be kept clean. A cotton bandana would do, or one of the elastic athletic type. They may be purchased in the proper colors or dyed, either method is acceptable.

White would be the basic color for the beginner, progressing to brown and then to black. A black and white headband would signify a senior student or a master, a warrior of the first rank. If a class were large enough to warrant such distinctions, an OD green headband would denote the instructors and a camouflage headband would denote senior students or the master of the hall. These things should be worked out organically within the class.

The white ranking would begin with basic techniques (see the training schedule in the last chapter) taught by constant repetition. Physical training is not overly emphasized here, just the learning of the technique. As the student progresses, the demands made on him for stamina and conditioning are greater. More repetitions are taught.

At the brown level the grappling and other advanced skills are introduced as well as more physical training and conditioning. He must be able to move fluidly in attack and defense as well as fight using combinations. As he progresses at this level, basic skills are retaught and honed to perfection. Weaponry is introduced in special classes for the senior ranks.

At the black level the student should have a firm grasp of all of the techniques outlined in this manual, and be reasonably proficient in their use. The instructors come from this rank level and in teaching others they teach themselves. If they had to, they could teach themselves from this rank on because of their mastery of the basics.

The Instructor

The warrior way is for self-defense of the individual and others. As such, its training methods are to place the individual in one stressful situation after another and teach him to cope by relying on the methods of the way. It is in the life-or-death struggle that the warrior way has its roots, not in any sporting event. One must be conscious of the purpose of training; sometimes it is strict, disciplined, even severe. There is a point to it, however.

The instructor, regardless of rank, must push his students physically to new levels of attainment. He must instill the spirit of a warrior during training, occasionally making his advanced students feel that their personal well-being is in danger, then allowing them to alleviate that danger by the use of good technique. The more advanced a student becomes, the more often threatened. He must be forced to feel danger and exhaustion, but he must be allowed to overcome it, not be discouraged by reaching his physical limits. The instructor must ensure this, and end each training session on a positive note.

The student must experience fear and worry to overcome them. In a controlled atmosphere he may overcome them through training without serious injury or loss of life, building confidence and emotional strength through the experience. This is the main task of the instructor; anything less would cheat the student.

There is no place in the student, the instructor, or the training hall for fragile egos or foolish pride. On the other hand, a bully will find that he has no place in martial arts either. Cooperation between the students is essential for an orderly training session. When paired with a training partner, cooperate with him. If the instructor asks you to perform a technique, do so. It is his duty to teach you, but it is your duty to be attentive and to learn.

Terminology

When Karate was transplanted from Okinawa to Japan early in this century, the Okinawan master who brought it over, Dr. Funakoshi Gichin, changed much of the terminology so that it would better suit the Japanese. Apparently this did not harm the art itself in any form. Therefore, since this manual is written in a predominately English-speaking country, the terminology used here is what might better suit an English-speaking warrior. The individual techniques are named as they are presented.

Listed here are some of the general terms used and their descriptions:

Strategy — Overall plan for victory; selection of plans, priorities, etc.

Tactics — Specific methods of accomplishing the strategy.

(EXAMPLES: *Strategy:* destroy opponent's morale; his will to win or continue.

Tactics: break his balance with low kicks and foot sweeps; spring unexpected ambushes in combat.)

Striking Point or Area — Specific part of the body that makes contact during the execution of a technique (the two foreknuckles in a straight punch for example).

Vital Point — The specific area of your opponent's body to be attacked.

Target Area — General area of your opponent to attack (the hand, shin, etc.).

Lead Side — In a stance, whichever side is forward or closest to the opponent.

Reverse Side — In a stance, whichever side is back or furthest from the opponent.

Strong Side — For a right-handed person, their right side.

Weak Side — For a right-handed person, their left side. Both of these refer to a non-trained martial artist, who should have no strong or weak sides.

Bioenergy — The inexplicable Force that is within us all; the vital life force.

Chapter Four

Strategies and Tactics

Blending what the senses perceive, how the mind translates those perceptions, and your martial training into proper action is not easy. One must be aware of what is going on around him at all times, especially during a confrontation or fight, and not be so absorbed in one single process that he misses other crucial activities around him. Persons that want to hurt you give subtle hints of those emotions and such hints may be perceived. There are exercises listed in this section that allow the limbic portion of the brain, the area some researchers feel is responsible for extended sensory perception, to work freely. This may be developed with training.

This section deals with methods to integrate the functions of the body and the brain in stress-related situations so that you become one smoothly flowing unit, not two working independently of each other. It requires that you cultivate the proper attitudes, foresight and sensitivity that cause you to seemingly be in the right place at the right time. This is not luck, but planning and intuition in a warrior, understanding the situation and acting on it.

The object of martial training is not simply to memorize techniques so that they may be repeated by rote when you fight, but to make them part of yourself. When you sleep you breathe without conscious thought; equally the goal of training is that when you must fight you do so without conscious thought. You create the harmony between the two means of action, discipline and intuition, through training. You learn the physical mechanics and the methods in training, but if you do not make them a part of yourself and if you stop training, forgetfulness and time will cause you to lose much of what you have learned.

The methods in this chapter allow one to reawaken abilities that lie dormant in most people. Martial arts are a skill that man has always known, like swimming, but has lost through domesticity. Not the exact techniques, perhaps, but the skills associated with empty-hand fighting, including mental perceptions that we have no use for in this modern society. Perhaps the time has come to reawaken these skills.

Body Zoning

The body is divided into three horizontal levels and one vertical line for centering yourself with the opponent. The vertical line is the most important for positioning in offense or defense. The three horizontal levels are used for recognition of technique.

The High Level — begins at the base of the neck and extends upward as far as your arms reach. This forms the upper defensive perimeter. This level must be guarded by the peripheral vision as well as the head's natural ability to move from side to side and from front to rear. One hand also guards the head and high level.

The Mid Level — begins at the base of the neck and extends downward to a point one inch below the navel. It also extends outward from the torso in all directions as far as the arms will reach, forming the mid level defensive perimeter. This area must be guarded with peripheral vision; the elbows and one hand form a guard, and the ability to move the torso by turning at the hips or stepping out of the way of an attack. The high level is smaller in area than the mid level making the mid level more susceptible to attack.

The Low Level — begins one inch below the navel and extends downward to the ground and outward in all directions as far as the legs will reach, forming the lower defensive perimeter. The low level is targeted to reduce mobility and must be guarded with peripheral vision and the natural ability of the legs to move away from attack.

The Center Line — is an imaginary line that extends from the top of your head to your feet, running through your groin, navel, throat, between your eyes and the center of your forehead when you are standing in a Ready stance facing your opponent. Many vital points are located along your center line. It must be guarded with the hands and the ability to step or turn away from attack at whichever level the attack comes. Striking to your opponent's center line is advised. Your focus in training should always be either your own or your training partner's center line. This will often force you to change position or stance to deliver the technique, but that is what the center line theory is for. Blocks should always pass through your own center line.

Outer Defensive Perimeter — When you are in a Fighting stance with your hands in a mid level guard, the outer defensive perimeter begins at the lead side elbow. It extends outward, toward your opponent. It is like an imaginary line running above your head to the ground through the elbow. This area is used in initial contact during a fight, and for long range fighting. When your opponent penetrates this, he is in your inner defensive perimeter.

Inner Defensive Perimeter — When you are in a Fighting stance with your hands in the mid level guard the inner defensive perimeter begins at your lead side elbow and extends backward from the elbow to your back. This area is where the real fighting occurs. Attacks are initiated in the outer defensive perimeter, but to finish the opponent you must close with him and penetrate his inner defensive perimeter with your techniques.

Closing the Gap — The distance between you and your opponent is called the gap. To get to him and end the fight you must effectively close that gap with your body, getting in position to penetrate his inner defensive perimeter and finish him. There are many methods of doing this, some of which are outlined in the technique sections, some of which you will learn in training for yourself. The most common method of closing the gap is to use a low kick, closing with hand or grappling techniques. Secondly, one may feign with the hand and attack with a kick. The third method is to evade or redirect the opponent's initial attack and use footwork to close the gap.

Range — In combat, distancing, the amount of range between you and your opponent is your first weapon. For your opponent to strike you, or for you to strike him, he must be within a certain range. Being able to recognize these ranges is critical for you. You must stop him from closing to his ideal range but be able to strike him at your ideal range. This is effected through a combination of evasion, blocking, footwork and training. When you are working with your training partner, observe how close you must be to him or he to you for your strikes to be effective. Try to stop him from hitting you by simply shifting out of his way. You will come to identify distancing quickly. It is especially important when fighting someone that knows how to kick.

Center Line

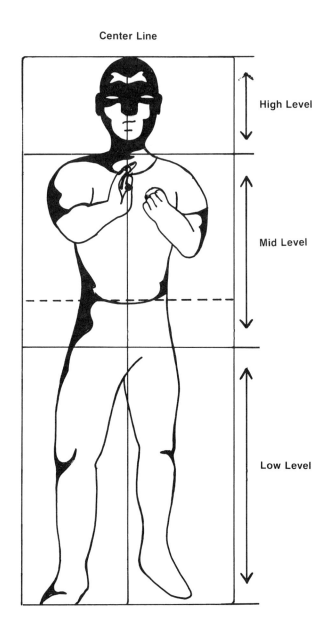

**Outer
Defensive Perimeter**

**Inner
Defensive Perimeter**

Center Line

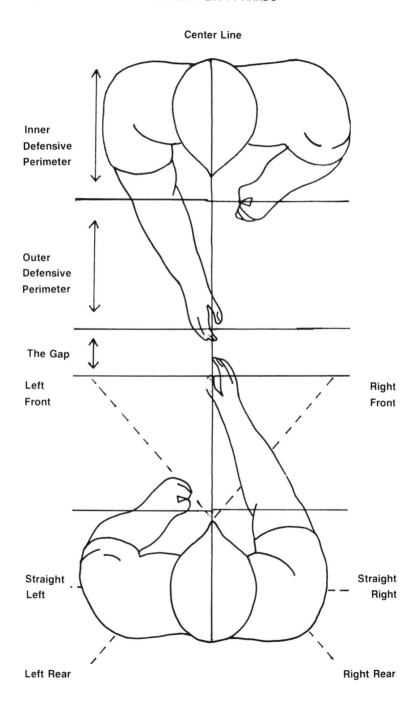

Inner
Defensive
Perimeter

Outer
Defensive
Perimeter

The Gap

Left
Front

Right
Front

Straight
Left

Straight
Right

Left Rear

Right Rear

Five Points of Attack

The five points of attack are the five directions or angles from which you may be attacked or may launch your own attacks. By being aware of these potential gaps in your own defense and learning to cover them with your guard and peripheral vision, your defense will be impervious. Conversely, when you see them as an opening in your opponent's defense, you will strike into them instantly.

Straight Ahead — From any level, a straight line to the target is the fastest, so it is the most common method used in striking.

Overhead — This is used in weapons strikes or when attacking with a bottom fist strike and is not often used as an initial attack.

Below — This attack usually comes from beneath your line of sight. Examples of an attack from below are a low front snap kick and an uppercut punch.

Left Side — This attack angles in from the flank as in a hooking punch or a round kick. It is often difficult to see, coming from a 'blind' spot.

Right Side — The same as the left side, examples of which would be a hook punch or a round kick. These circular attacks are very effective in combination.

Eight Points of Balance

These are the directions in which you may be off-balanced, or pull your opponent off balance. These will help you recognize when your opponent is off balance and in what direction, when he has over-extended himself in a technique, or when you have pulled him into such a position.

Straight Forward — He is leaning forward on the balls of both feet and will fall forward if given momentum in that direction.

Straight Backward — He is leaning backward on both heels, in extreme cases with his toes not touching the ground. He will fall backward with momentum in that direction.

Right Side — He is leaning on the outer edge of his right foot. He will fall easily to the right side with a shove in that direction.

Left Side — He is leaning to the left on the outer edge of his left foot.

Right Front — At about a forty-five degree angle to Forward Right. This brings the person onto the ball and the forward edge of the right foot just behind the little toe. He is easily tripped or swept to the right from this position.

Left Front — At about a forty-five degree angle to the Forward Left. This brings the person onto the ball and the forward edge of the left foot just behind the little toe. He is easily thrown or swept to his left from this point.

Right Rear — At about a forty-five degree angle to the right from Straight Back. This brings the person onto the outside rear edge of his left heel. The person is easily pushed over backward to his right from this point.

Left Rear — At about a forty-five degree angle to Straight Back, to the left. This brings the person onto the rear outer edge of his left foot. He is easily pushed backward to his left from this point.

To familiarize yourself with the eight points more thoroughly, assume a Ready stance with the feet parallel about shoulder width apart, hands relaxed at your sides. Lean your body forward from the waist upward until you have to balance on the balls of your feet to keep from falling. Observe your own body position and the loss of balance as you lean forward. Then rotate slightly to your right at about forty-five degrees until you are on the ball of your right foot and the outer edge just behind the little toe. Often people will come up on this edge to reach out and grab someone. Next lean straight to the right until you are on the edge of the right foot. Now rotate to about forty-five degrees to the right rear, coming up on the rear outer edge of the right heel. This is the position of off-balance used for rear reaps and sweeps, but often a strong push will put you in this position. Lean straight backward onto the rear edge of both heels. Continue for the left side points of balance, getting the feel of each. If it is possible, do this in front of a mirror, so that you can see the points as you reach them and are able to recognize them in an opponent when he off-balances himself. Do this rotation exercise slowly and try to lean as far into each point as you can without falling. There is a chart showing these points. You are standing in the center of the wheel in the chart, and the arrow indicates the direction of the point of balance.

Direction of Movement

There are eight directions of stepping used in description of technique in this manual, particularly in the stance section, that should be clarified. In actual fighting and free sparring there are numerous directions that one may step, but in training they are condensed into eight. In use, you step where your technique will do the most damage to your opponent; in combat everything is modified relative to your opponent's positioning and your angle of delivery.

These eight directions of movement are exactly the same as the eight points of balance. They use the same names. In the stance section, and where application of technique is described, foot placement comes into the direction of stepping also. To understand the basic reference, however, directions of movement are based theoretically on you facing your opponent squarely. In the chart, you are at the center of a circle facing your opponent squarely, in the direction of movement called Straight Forward. All of the other directions of movement are based on you moving from that circle.

For example, you face your opponent in a Ready stance and he rushes at you. Step to your right front (a forty-five degree angle to your right and forward from the straight line on which you had been facing him and along which he is rushing) with your right foot, avoiding his rush. If you are facing him and he attacks you with a left straight punch along your center line, you might bring the right foot to the left rear (a forty-five degree angle from the straight line you had been facing him on to your left and the rear) to slip the punch. Similarly, you might step to the left front with the left foot to slip a right punch from the opponent. There are countless examples of this in the stance and technique sections. A basic understanding is required for use when training in movement, though. Study the Chart and the charts in the other sections in relation to footwork and you will understand the eight directions of movement.

Angles of Movement

The eight points of balance and the eight angles of movement are basically the same and may be represented on one chart for simplification. To understand the chart, you are standing at the center of a circle with eight spokes radiating from it like the spokes from the hub of a wheel. The direction that the arrow points for each respective circle is the direction of movement to step, or to obtain a point of off balance.

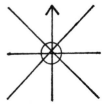

Straight Forward

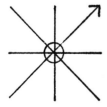

Right Forward

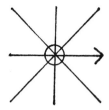

Straight Right

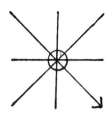

Right Rear

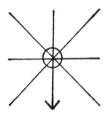

Straight Rear

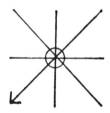

Left Rear

Straight Left

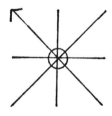

Left Forward

Peripheral Vision

You often hear the advice, "Watch his eyes", or his shoulders to observe the movements or predict the next strike of the opponent. This may be useful in a sporting situation where the opponent cannot kick you, but when he can and is willing to do so, watching his eyes is not that good of an idea. If you focus on the high level you cannot see what his low level is doing. To fully observe your own and his five points of attack you must lower your sight from his high level. The ideal spot is the area of his solar plexus. From this point you can observe the entire range of his movements with your peripheral vision. You will react much faster to the things seen in your periphery; combat troops are taught to observe areas with their peripheral vision and not stare into one area.

To better develop your awareness of peripheral vision, pick a spot off in the distance and stare at it. Move your hands to the limits of your peripheral vision and slowly move them in and out. Strain to see them when they move out of your range of vision, but *do not* move your eyes to the sides to follow them! It will be a temptation, but force your eyes to remain straight ahead. This discipline will help you keep your eyes focused on your opponent's solar plexus during a fight. The reason for this is to avoid reacting to a feint on his part. If you look in the direction of his feint, taking your eyes off of his solar plexus, his real attack may slip into a blind angle of attack, which he created with the feint.

Next, have your training partner stand in front of you at a little more than his arms' reach. Both of you assume Fighting stances. Have him attack you with various hand techniques, stopping just short of impact. You may slip or block his techniques, but be sure that you keep your eyes centered on his solar plexus. If he attempts to flank you, shift your stance so that your center line is still facing his and your eyes are still on his solar plexus. After you have some proficiency at this, have him include kicking attacks to your low and mid levels with the hand techniques, so that you are used to seeing *all* five points of attack, and being threatened in *all* three levels with your peripheral vision. Look for openings in his attacks with your peripheral vision as you slip or block his attacks.

The Guard

There are essentially two methods of guarding the body that keep the hands, arms, and elbows in ideal position to block most attacks to the high or mid level. Because fights are usually conducted at varying ranges, no one guard position is ideal. In the long range and middle range, one type of guard is required; in the close range, another type of guard becomes more effective.

Mid Level Guard — This is used for long and mid range fighting distances. It keeps the elbows close to the torso for defense, yet keeps the hands and arms out far enough to intercept attacks before they enter your inner defensive perimeter. Form a left leg leading Fighting stance (see the stance section). The right reverse arm is held with the fist clenched and is used for countering attacks. The fist is roughly level with the bottom of the chin, right elbow tucked into the right ribs or hip. Keep the head erect, chin lowered forward very slightly. When you strike with either arm, turn the chin into that shoulder so that if the opponent counters to the high level as you strike, your lower jaw and throat will be protected. The leading left hand is open or closed as you feel inclined. It is held at mid bicep height, extended forward with the arm bent so that the forearm forms roughly a ninety degree angle to the upper arm. Keep the elbow in close to the torso, not bowed outward. The lead hand should be held at your own center line, not off to the side of it. The elbows, in this guard, work as an axis for blocks.

This guard is reversed when you change into a right side leading Fighting stance, or any other stance for that matter.

Close Range Guard — Assume a left side leading Fighting stance with your hands in the Mid Level Guard. Lower your left leading hand with the fist opened and the palm turned to the ground between your legs. The elbow is slightly bent, arm held close to the body, the hand cocked back and up so that the palm is exposed to the ground. Move your right hand to the left side of your face, near your left shoulder with the hand open and the palm turned to the left. Keep the elbow close to the torso and keep it bent. The left hand is at your own groin height and the right hand is approximately at your own jaw height, no further from your face than the outside of the left shoulder. This is reversed when you shift into a right stance.

The mid level guard is used for initial contact and fighting when you have room to maneuver, keeping your opponent away from you with kicks and lead hand strikes. It is very effective when fighting an opponent that kicks, or against boxers. It may also be used against armed opponents. The close range guard is used when you are engaged in an area where you cannot move around, or when the opponent and you are in close contact, for in-fighting techniques. Both guard positions are effective, allowing rapid deployment of either arm for any level strike or block.

If you face a martial artist in self-defense or combat and the opponent begins making exotic movements with his hands, or ferocious faces, ignore them. Much of this was originally designed to intimidate the average opponent who had no knowledge of martial arts. Keeping the lead hand in subtle motion is effective to distract the opponent, allowing you to attack with another limb, or to cover the actual line of attack with the lead hand. Usually that is not necessary, unless your opponent has been particularly well-trained.

If your opponent begins to pose in strange stances, makes strange noises, or begins displaying flowery hand movements, ignore them. He does not know arcane or superior fighting methods than yours. Keep your guard alert, stay prepared, and if he crosses into your outer defensive perimeter at proper range, strike him powerfully in the mid level. He will probably stop doing all of these strange motions at this time and either fight or leave, excusing himself for being stupid as he does so.

Physical Principles

When a trained martial artist says, "My body is a weapon", he is often taken to mean that his hands and feet are able to damage or even kill an opponent. This interpretation is valid, though it is not the essence of the saying. One may truly convert his entire body into a weapon through the use of three physical principles.

The first is the gradual release of power called **acceleration.** It is subdivided into two elements: relaxation of the muscles involved in the specific technique, and coordinated body shifting.

To describe the principle we shall view it in action, in a reverse punch. The reverse punch is one of the strongest punches because the rear leg is used to thrust the technique forward. It is launched from the non-leading side in any stance and is often used as a counter punch after blocking or evading your opponent's first strike.

Assume a left Fighting stance with your hands in a mid level guard. Relax all of the muscles in your body. Breathe deeply. Concentrate on performing only this technique. Cock your hips slightly to the right rear. Suddenly snap your right leg straight, pushing your right hip forward, and shift into a left Front stance. This begins the crucial forward rotation of your hip. Snap it into the forward motion; the hip is the fulcrum of power in all techniques. As the hip rotates forward, turn your right shoulder forward. Bring the arm forward in a straight line, keeping the elbow in close to the torso and not letting it angle outward. It is essential that you stay relaxed throughout this movement. Just before your vertical fist strikes its target, you must lock your wrist and tense the fist tightly.

Your fist in this thrust is like the weighted end of a whip, even though the technique moves straight forward. Its mass gradually picks up momentum until it reaches peak velocity. If you tense your muscles during the acceleration phase of the thrust you will produce friction and slow the thrust down, not allowing it to reach its full potential. Relaxed muscles cause little drag.

The second principle occurs as the fist strikes the target. It is called **focus** and is subdivided into two elements also. One is penetration, attempting to drive your technique to a certain depth in or through your opponent. Even if the technique itself does not penetrate, the shock waves will. The second subdivision is tension at the moment of penetration; bringing your entire body to complete tension, exhaling sharply, projecting your emotional strength into the blow.

As the reverse punch strikes the target, the torqueing effect of acceleration is over. Your muscles are no longer capable of producing momentum. At the instant of penetration you must tense your entire body to produce force and impart it to the opponent. Begin by exhaling sharply from the lower diaphragm upward, bringing the lower torso to tension. Tighten all of the muscles in your body as you exhale. By giving a verbal spirit shout you project your fighting spirit, your will to win, and some of your emotional energy into the technique as well.

This sudden tension provides the shock force, the snap, to the technique. Without that focus and tension it would only be a hard push, an arm punch, and not a body punch. As your skill in this principle increases, the time that you stay tensed should decrease. It only takes a second of tension when the technique is delivered. Relax again completely, and quickly withdraw the punch to the chambered position of the mid level guard. By immediate retrieval you are chambered for a follow-up technique with the lead side. More importantly, you move your fist away from the shock waves you have just delivered into your opponent. The blow implodes into/through him rather than exploding on the surface, which causes much less damage.

The crucial element to focus is proper distancing for your penetration. Ideally, at the moment of tension, your punching arm should not be fully extended and locked out. It should remain partially bent at the elbow. This means that you must be within proper range, close enough to assure penetration, yet far enough away that you do make contact while body shifting is still developing, jamming the punch.

It comes with practice.

The third principle is **speed of delivery.** Speed should be developed through both strengthening the muscles used in a given technique, and by keeping them very flexible. This reduces the drag created by friction also. Tight or tense muscles drag on the striking limb, causing inertia, reducing speed.

The force of any technique is measured by its ability to accelerate mass; in this case, your opponent's mass. Most of the force that is delivered on target is the result of momentum created during the acceleration process. The part of your body that strikes your opponent after it accelerates out of the chamber becomes a projectile much like a bullet once its powder charge is ignited, propelling it out of the chamber. The greater the initial momentum the more energy on target.

For a set mass (your arm in a reverse punch), doubling its momentum will quadruple your speed.

In a fluid combat situation where your opponent is able to move freely (unlike a punching bag in the training hall) a slow, powerful technique is not efficient. Your opponent may evade it, roll with it, step inside it, and jam it. If it lands it will only be a rough push. You must use your distancing as a weapon too, and move decisively when you attack. The greater the speed of delivery, the more probable it is that your technique will accelerate his mass beyond the ability of his built-in cushioning (muscles, skin tissue, etc.) to protect less flexible centers (bones, joints, etc.). This is how blocking technique may be used to break bones in the offending limb of the opponent, bearing out the precept: Defense and Offense are One.

These principles may only be mastered through repetitive practice. Once they are mastered, the body, not just the limbs, is a weapon.

Vital Striking Points

The study of vital striking points in the martial arts is very old, as noted in the first chapter. Since martial arts have become so popular around the world, many studies have been done on the human anatomy; physiologists have given us volumes of knowledge on the strengths and weaknesses of the body. Based on this modern anatomical knowledge the vital striking points and the results of striking them are listed below.

The assumption for this section is that the blow delivered to each area is delivered properly, with full force and focus, accurately on target. Because of the varying strength of individuals and the fluidity of real combat, the results are listed from minor to major. If you miss the exact target area but still land a solid blow you will do damage; perhaps not the exact damage you had intended, but sufficient to end a fight. In martial arts a near miss may be as devastating as a direct hit.

Too often a martial artist will throw seven or eight blows that land but do not stop a fight, or stand and exchange blows with an adversary. This shows a lack of training in the vital striking points. In combat, or if the opponent is armed, you may have time to land only one or two blows, and they must be telling blows. Knowing where to strike often is as important as knowing how. Learning these vital striking points will enable you to end fights quickly.

1. Crown of the head — just behind hairline; the coronal structure, area of juncture of the frontal bones and the parietal bones.
Effects:
- unconsciousness due to great shock to the cranial nerves, a possible fracture of the natural fault line of the skull;
- death due to fracture of the fault line causing internal bleeding and shock.

2. Top of the head — frontal fontanel, the region of the head between the forehead and the coronal suture that is exposed and seen pulsating in newborn children.
Effects:
- unconsciousness due to concussion, the brain being slammed against the cranial walls, shock to the cranial nerve;
- rupture of the fault line causing internal bleeding and death.

3. Forehead — between the hairline and the bridge of the nose.
Effects:
- rupture of blood vessels close to the surface of the skin causing swelling of the eyes;
- concussion causing brain damage, blood clots, unconsciousness from the brain being slammed against the cranial walls;
- fracture of the frontal bone or the sinus cavity causing bone fragment to enter the brain, piercing the dura. This leads to brain damage or death.

4. Temple — the suture of the cheek bones and frontal bones, the area directly behind the eyes.
Effects:
- fracture of the temporal region, severing the meningeal artery.

The meningeal artery supplies blood to the skull and the membrane that covers the brain, the dura; it follows the groove along the inner temple. A severed artery causes coma and probably death.

- a bursting fracture along the natural fault line. The temporal bone is located between the natural fault lines between the temporal and sphenoid lobes. This could lead to bone fragments entering the brain itself; rupturing the dura; concussion and shock leading to death.

5. Circumorbital Region — Upper and lower parts of the eye sockets; the cheek bones.

Effects:

- uncontrolled watering of the eyes;
- fracture of the cheek bones causing shock and possible loss of consciousness due to great pain;
- trauma to the brain and the resulting loss of nervous control.

6. Eyes — the bulbs of both eyes.

Effects:

- at least uncontrolled watering of both eyes even if only one is struck, which causes temporary loss of vision;
- collapsed bulb of the eye leading to shock and permanent blindness, great pain.

7. Ears — the area of the ears, inner and outer.

Effects:

- concussion from the force of the blow to the head;
- rupture of the eardrum from a large volume of air being forced through the auditory canal into a much smaller space. With rupture of the eardrum comes loss of hearing and equilibrium and great pain.

8. Bridge of the nose — the glabella, point between the eyes where the nose joins the forehead.

Effects:

- fracture of the nasal bone and the septum causing massive hemorrhage, massive shock, temporary blindness from severe watering of the eyes;
- severe trauma to cerebrum; as in most head strikes disruptive stimulation of the cranial nerves and loss of sensory and motor function leading to unconsciousness.

9. Philtrum — juncture of the left and right jaw bones below the nose, and just inside the tip of the nose.

Effects:

- traumatic pain and damage to the septum and cartilage; uncontrolled watering of the eyes from damage to nerve clusters in the nose; possible loss of teeth, split lip, ruptured blood vessels causing hematoma. The cluster of small nerves under the lip and in the tip of the nose make this a particularly sensitive area;

- bursting fracture of the upper jaw if the angle of the blow is not directed upward leading to severe pain and unconsciousness. The skull is spherical in shape and will only compress so far before it bursts open. The fracture point is slightly to one side or the other of the impact point;

- severe trauma to the cranial nerves and unconsciousness; respiratory paralysis and death; broken teeth and blood from ruptured vessels may be caught in or near the trachea causing muscular spasms in the vocal cord closing off the air supply leading to death.

10. Lower Mandible — approximately one-half inch beneath the lower lip.

Effects:

- traumatic pain, possible loss of teeth, laceration of lip and ruptured blood vessels leading to hematoma;

- bursting fracture of the lower jaw leading to shock unconsciousness;

- severe trauma to the cranial nerves leading to unconsciousness.

11. Jaw — mandible base, the lower ridge of the jaw and the articulation below and in front of both ears.

Effects:

- severe trauma to the cranial nerves causing unconsciousness;

- fracture or dislocation of the lower jaw (i.e. separation of the lower jaw bone from the cartilage of the maxillary hinge) and connected watering of the eyes;

- localized fracture of the jaw itself at the point of impact;

- fracture of the cheek bones if the force of the blow is directed upward or misses the lower ridge.

12. Side of the neck — the length of the sternomastoid muscle covered by the platysma.

Effects:

- a soft strike to the platysma and the sternomastoid muscles on the side of the neck will cause the throat to contract. A hard strike may penetrate to the hyoid bone in the throat rupturing the trachea and causing nerve damage, rupturing the jugular vein and carotid artery causing at least temporary loss of blood to the brain. A possible rupture of the jugular or carotid is serious and could lead to death;
- muscular spasms of the above muscles after a non-penetrating strike which will clamp off the jugular vein and carotid artery, shutting off the blood to the brain. Any damage to the jugular or carotid may cause thrombosis (blood clot) and require surgery to correct;
- compression and damage to the nerves in the front of the throat; rupture of the thyroid gland causing loss of consciousness and choking.

13. Front of the throat — supraclavicular fossa, front of the throat on either side just above the collar bones at the origin of the head of the sternomastoid muscle.

Effects:

- trauma to the artery located below the collar bone (subclavian artery) and to the sublingual nerve producing shock and loss of motor function.

14. Suprasternal Notch — the juncture of the collar bones, a concavity on the ventral surface of the neck between the sternum below and the sternohyoid muscle above.

Effects:

- fracture of the collar bones (clavicles) causing pain and loss of use of the arm on the side of the fracture;
- possible penetration of the larynx by bone fragments resulting in internal bleeding;
- blockage of the trachea shutting off the respiratory process, causing severe choking if the air passage is not cleared; death can result.

15. Behind the ears — concavity behind the ears between the mastoid process and the lower jaw.

Effects:

- severe trauma to the cranial nerves and spinal cord, unconsciousness due to severe jarring of the brain against the cranial walls;
- concussion; a blow to this part of the head can snap the head at an angle and sever a vertebra or crack the skull itself;
- severe trauma to the small nerve clusters near the surface.

16. Nape of the neck — third invertebral space, from the center of the skull to the base of the neck.

Effects:

- severe trauma to the cerebrum, cranial nerves and spinal cord;
- muscle spasms and whiplash, concussion from the shock waves of the blow which may cause death;
- severed vertebra to broken neck with paralysis; if the cord is severed above the fifth cervical vertebra death will result, as this cuts the phrenic nerve which controls the function of the diaphragm in breathing;
- multiple fractures of the spinal cord which also may damage the phrenic nerve and cause paralysis or at least unconsciousness.

17. Collar bones — clavicles running from the sternum to the shoulders.

Effects:

- severance or laceration of the brachial nerve plexus and subclavian artery, causing paralysis to the arm with possible gangrene or internal bleeding;
- fracture of the clavicle itself, causing severe pain and temporary loss of use of the arm on the side of the fracture, as well as all of the above;
- puncture of a lung by bone fragments from a fracture of a clavicle.

18. Summit of the Sternum — at the junction of the clavicles and chest plate.

Effects:

- fracture of the tips of the clavicles and severe pain, loss of breath; bone fragments being forced inward from the fracture to the lower area of the trachea;
- fracture of the upper sternum causing pain, loss of breath, and

possibly penetration of the lungs by bone fragments. This may lead to the lungs collapsing.

19. Sternum — just below the juncture of the manubrium and the sternum, the chest plate itself.

Effects:

- severe shock to the heart, lungs, and the pulmonary artery leading to malfunction of the respiratory system and shock;
- actually breaking the sternum, forcing bone fragments into the organs of the chest cavity, leading to internal bleeding and severe shock.

20. Base of the Sternum — the xiphoid process, lowest part of the sternum.

Effects:

- the xiphoid is a soft bone at the tip of the sternum that is easily broken and pushed inward. Depending on the angle of the strike it may rupture several of the organs of the chest cavity and cause severe shock;
- severe trauma to the organs of the chest cavity even if the xiphoid is not broken. It is nearly impossible to build muscle up over this area to protect it. A hard blow may collapse a lung without breaking the xiphoid.

21. Below the Nipples — below the nipples between the fifth and sixth ribs on either side; in the front directly below the nipples.

Effects:

- the left side is directly over the heart. Blows to that area will at least cause loss of breath and pain, though it may also shift the heart, causing death;
- on the right side the impact area is over the lungs which may collapse with the loss of breath and consciousness, possibly death.

22. Ribs — from armpit to waist line.

Effects:

- fifth rib below armpit, the subaxillary region; loss of breath due to relaxation of the muscles between each rib forcing air out of the lungs, causing unconsciousness; rupture of organs in the area, including the lungs; broken or fractured ribs forcing jagged ends inward into organs and rupturing them, leading to internal bleeding and severe shock;

- seventh and eighth ribs of the abdomen, the hypochondriac region; on the right side severe trauma to the liver leading to loss of motor function associated with liver and lungs; on the left side severe trauma to the stomach and spleen with effects on the heart and lungs, producing loss of motor function in those organs leading to shock; damage such as a fracture to the bones of the ribs leading to jagged ends or bone splinters being forced inward into organs leading to rupture of those organs, internal bleeding, shock, death;
- abdomen, lumbar region, ninth, tenth, eleventh ribs; on the left is the spleen which will rupture due to severe compression which leads to shock, loss of blood, unconsciousness; coma and even death; fracture of the ribs forcing jagged ends or splinters into the spleen leading to the same results; on the right side it is nearly the same as the above.

23. Diaphragm — front of the abdomen from the lower sternum to the umbilicus (navel) including the stomach.
Effects:
- loss of breath due to sudden relaxation of the muscles between the ribs, forcing air out of the lungs causing unconsciousness;
- rupture of organs in the stomach cavity due to compression, causing shock, internal bleeding, unconsciousness, possibly death.

24. Bladder — approximately one and a half inches below the umbilicus.
Effects:
- trauma to the small intestine and bladder and in turn to the large blood vessels and nerves in the lower abdomen producing severe shock;
- rupture of the bladder releasing urine into the body cavity;
- fracture of the pubic bone with a possibility for the bone to puncture intestines producing hemorrhage and shock.

25. Kidney — area of the lower back slightly off center from the spine on each side.
Effects:
- compression of the organ with possible rupture causing severe pain and shock, internal bleeding, coma and possibly death;
- broken ribs with the jagged ends piercing the organs produc-

ing the same results as above;

- shock waves continuing into the body cavity causing disruption of other organs in the lower abdomen.

26. Groin — area between the thighs, including the testicles.
Effects:
- severe trauma to the nerves of the testicles and groin shutting off the respiratory system and inducing severe nausea;
- rupture of the testes causing intense pain, shock, vomiting, unconsciousness, and even death from shock;
- fracture of the pubic bone that could penetrate the bladder or the intestines.

27. Scapular ridge — between the shoulder blades, the level of the third intercostal space.
Effects:
- trauma to the lungs and spinal column causing loss of breath and temporary paralysis;
- whiplash effect radiating pain through the back and pinched nerve roots causing partial paralysis which may be permanent.

28. Middle of the back — between the fifth and sixth thoracic vertebra.
Effects:
- trauma to the spinal cord, aorta, and the lungs leading to loss of sensory and motor functions and stoppage of breath;
- fracture of the thoracic vertebra causing paralysis from the point of the fracture downward.

29. Lower back — lumbar region of the back, left and right sides of the ninth and eleventh vertebra.
Effects:
- severe trauma to the kidneys and associated nerve and blood vessels leading in turn to shock and loss of motor function (see kidney);
- fracture of the lumbar vertebrae causing intense pain and partial paralysis from the point of the fracture downward.

30. Tip of the spine — the coccyx.
Effects:
- trauma to the entire spinal cord leading to cerebral trauma;

- traumatic pain from the break which is not incapacitating in itself but causes so much pain from movement that it will end a fight due to shock.

31. Lower buttocks — gluteal fold, the central portion of the back of the upper thigh just below the buttock.
Effects:

- trauma to the sciatic nerve producing an unusual type of pain in the abdomen and hip region and loss of motor function.

32. Shoulder joints — area of the top of the ball and socket joint of the shoulders.
Effects:

- when the arm is stretched, under strain, or extended, a blow may smash the joint itself or dislocate it. This leads to loss of use of that arm and intense pain and shock.

33. Elbow joints — area of the back of the elbow joint itself.
Effects:

- when the joint is straight or under strain it may be dislocated, or the tendons in the joint and leading to the bicep muscle may be torn;
- fracture of the humerus, the large bone in the upper arm.

34. Inside of the wrist — between the brachioradialis and flexor muscles of the fingers.
Effects:

- an attack to this point produces trauma to the underlying nerve and artery leading to an unusual type of pain affecting the chest and throat regions causing loss of motor functions;
- numbness in the hand and temporary loss of use of that hand.

35. Back of the hand — especially points between the thumb and index fingers and between middle and ring fingers.
Effects:

- severe shock to the medial nerves leading to an unusual type of pain in the chest and throat region that produces loss of motor function. A similar result is to be expected from striking any of the bones in the back of the hand;
- fracture of one of the bones of the back of the hand resulting in the loss of use of that hand to grasp and sometimes strike.

36. Inner thigh — inguinal region of the upper, inner thigh.
Effects:
- this area is part of the musculature of the pubic bones. Trauma to the underlying nerve and femoral artery;
- this produces an unusual type of pain by closing off nerve centers in the hip and abdomen causing loss of motor function;
- dislocation of the hip leading to loss of use of that leg, severe shock and unconsciousness.

37. Side of the thigh — lateral part of the thigh, middle of the lateral vastus muscle.
Effects:
- dislocation of the hip joint, which like the shoulder is a ball and socket joint, causing severe pain and shock and the loss of use of that leg;
- torn muscles and spasms, temporary loss of use of the leg. There are several clusters of nerves in this area near the surface that can be traumatized by a blow to this area also producing an unusual pain in the hip and lower abdomen;
- fracture of the femur causing pain and shock and definite loss of use of the leg.

38. Knee joint — the front and sides of the joint itself.
Effects:
- a sprain, torn ligaments or muscles, torn cartilage all resulting in the loss of use of the joint;
- fracture of the femur and tibia or fibula, all causing severe shock and resulting in the loss of use of the leg.

39. Shin — front of the leg between shin and ankle, middle fibula.
Effects:
- severe lacerations and swelling;
- trauma to the fibular nerve which lies close to the skin as it is forced against the bone leading to severe pain;
- fracture of the fibula or the tibia.

40. Top of the foot — medial melleolus, the point just below the medial tuberosity of the tibia, a point on the surface of the tarsal bone just below the ankle at the front of the foot.
Effects:
- trauma to the tibial artery causing an unusual type of pain in the hip area leading to loss of motor function;

- dislocation or serious sprain of the ankle causing pain and loss of mobility;
- fracture of ankle joint causing severe pain and shock; fracture of the tip of the tibia causing pain and severe shock; both lead to loss of use of that foot.

41. Instep — medial portion of the top of the foot.
Effects:
- the main point of attack is slightly to the inside of the medial line between the tendons of the big toe and second toe. Severe trauma to the nerve located in the inside portion of the ankle instep, the tibial artery, and the deep fibular nerve causing an unusual type of pain in the leg, hip and abdomen leading to loss of motor function and unconsciousness;
- fracture of the small bones in the foot, the metatarsals, loss of use of the foot and severe pain.

42. Top of the foot — just below the heads of the metatarsals, top lateral portion of the foot between the ankle and the instep.
Effects:
- same as in the above.

43. Outer arm — dorsal surface of the upper arm, the area between the bicep and the tricep, inner and outer.
Effects:
- trauma to the ulnar nerve, the median nerve, and blood vessels of the upper arm, producing an unusual type of pain in the upper arm, chest and neck causing loss of motor function;
- muscle spasms and loss of use of the arm.

44. Back of upper arm — between the tricep muscles slightly above the elbow.
Effects:
- traumatic pain from the nerve clusters close to the skin at the juncture of the muscles; partial paralysis of the arm due to muscle spasms.

45. Back of lower arm — area where the forearm muscles split, just below the elbow.
Effects:
- traumatic pain from nerve clusters close to the surface of the

skin producing an unusual type of pain much as in the upper arm;

- fracture of the radius and ulna in the lower arm causing severe pain and loss of use of that hand; partial paralysis if not fracture.

46. Wrist — dorsal surface of the wrist, the space between the ends of the radius and the ulna.

Effects:

- trauma to the median nerve and loss of motor function of that hand;
- if the wrist is jammed back on itself at this point with a strong blow the joint may be shattered; fracture of the tips of the radius and ulna; both causing severe shock and loss of use of that hand.

A blow to any of the vital points of the face causes trauma to the cranial nerves resulting in loss of nervous coordination and consciousness as well as vascular shock. There are twelve cranial nerves possessing sensory, motor, or mixed functions and they offer a variety of methods to stun or knock your opponent unconscious, or in the last resort, to kill him.

Attacks to vital points located in the upper abdomen will result in primary trauma to internal organs with disruptive effects to the spinal cord and sympathetic nervous systems. This in turn affects cranial nerves, leading to loss of consciousness caused by shock and loss of sensory and motor functions and consequent stoppage of breathing. It is noteworthy in this connection that attacks to vital points located in the head do not always lead to loss of breathing in spite of loss of sensory and motor function.

By selection of a target area instead of a blind strike one may avoid damaging their own hand or foot, and have much better results when they strike. It is your duty to learn these vital striking points and practice them as well as your own accuracy in daily training. Being accurate is essential to the delivery of effective technique.

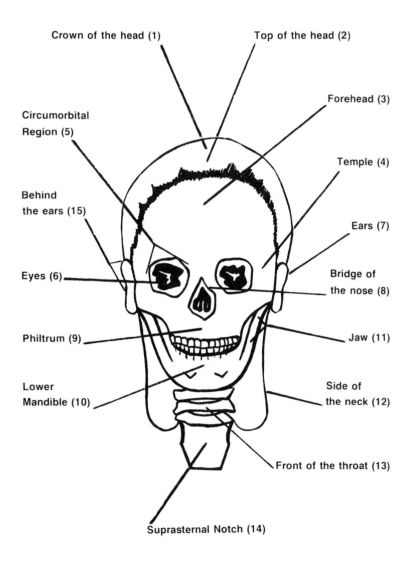

Crown of the head (1)

Top of the head (2)

Forehead (3)

Circumorbital
Region (5)

Temple (4)

Behind
the ears (15)

Ears (7)

Eyes (6)

Bridge of
the nose (8)

Philtrum (9)

Jaw (11)

Lower
Mandible (10)

Side of
the neck (12)

Front of the throat (13)

Suprasternal Notch (14)

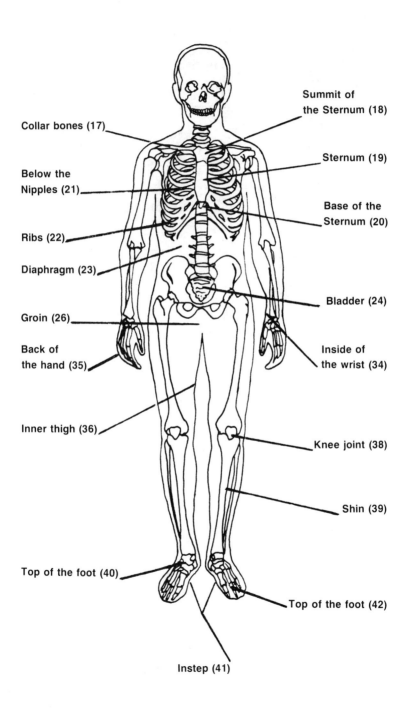

Summit of
the Sternum (18)

Sternum (19)

Collar bones (17)

Base of the
Sternum (20)

Below the
Nipples (21)

Ribs (22)

Diaphragm (23)

Bladder (24)

Groin (26)

Back of
the hand (35)

Inside of
the wrist (34)

Inner thigh (36)

Knee joint (38)

Shin (39)

Top of the foot (40)

Top of the foot (42)

Instep (41)

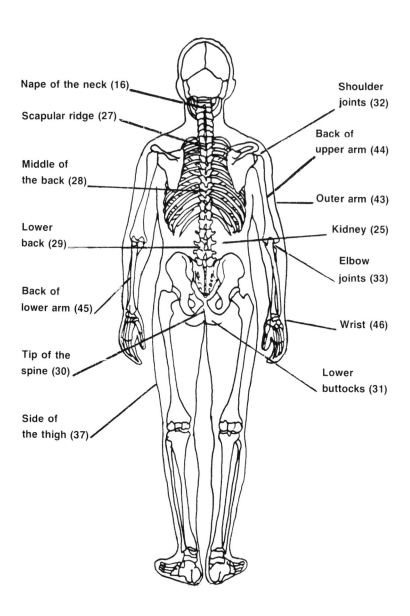

Nape of the neck (16)

Scapular ridge (27)

Middle of
the back (28)

Lower
back (29)

Back of
lower arm (45)

Tip of the
spine (30)

Side of
the thigh (37)

Shoulder
joints (32)

Back of
upper arm (44)

Outer arm (43)

Kidney (25)

Elbow
joints (33)

Wrist (46)

Lower
buttocks (31)

The Spirit Shout

In every martial training system in the world, including the military, the student is taught to expel breath vigorously when attacking, usually in the form of a battle roar. It serves to focus your concentration and your will on your opponent and, as a by-product, but not less important, on your technique. It serves to bring your diaphragm to tension at the moment of impact, thus tensing the entire body as explained in Physical Principles, to channel your bioenergy into the technique, and to off balance your opponent psychologically.

A warrior's spirit shout is different from the variety of other sounds heard in a fight. It projects the essence of the warrior, his fighting spirit, emotionally at the opponent. It must be spontaneous and come from the diaphragm to serve the purpose it is intended for. When you train, practice forcefully expelling air hard when you strike and tense. It need not be loud or any particular word, just empty the lower abdomen forcefully. Of course, you may shout if you choose. Channel your emotions as well as your physical strength into the exhalation.

Properly done, the spirit shout will develop the area of the lower abdomen and diaphragm. It is a form of dynamic tension training and will develop your striking power physically, when performed often. When you are straining physically at any time, at the moment of the greatest strain, perform a spirit shout, releasing all of your power at once.

The sound itself will affect your opponent. Everyone but the deaf are affected by loud noises, particularly if they are violent and unexpected. Sound is physical vibration in the air; when someone speaks to you, the air in front of his mouth is compressed which pushes the vibrations from molecule to molecule causing compression and expansion in the air. This finally hits your eardrum and causes it to vibrate. These vibrations are transmitted to your brain and interpreted. Since a sound is made up of three components, the auditory range is not able to select what it will hear and is therefore the victim of loud, sharp noises as they occur.

The three components of sound are pitch, volume and timbre. Pitch is the range the sound is heard on; how high or low on the scale of cycles per second, how many sound waves hit your ear over a given period of time. Volume is measured in decibels which vary according to the size of the sound wave hitting your ear. Timbre is how the sound wave resonates. That is, for example, how you tell the difference between a Harley Davidson and a Suzuki. When a sound wave hits an object it can change that object by making its molecules vibrate at

a different rate. That is how a human voice can shatter a glass. It
is a documented fact that a human voice can affect physical objects.
Cantors in the Greek Orthodox cathedrals have been known to snuff
out candles that were shielded from expulsion of air by individuals
as they canted, and the vibrations have shattered windows and crack-
ed eardrums. A warrior can, by experimenting, find the right combination of the three elements of the spirit shout to develop the right
pitch, volume, and timbre which are destructive to physical objects.
Emotional content plays a large part in a fighting situation when you
are releasing your bioenergy into the shout. If one can alter the flow
of the opponent's neural messages, one may subdue him without
violence; this is theoretically possible since all matter is made up of
vibrations from the rhythm inherent in atomic structure. In the Orient
there are schools devoted to the spirit shout, to both heal and kill.

Train in the use of a spontaneous, lusty spirit shout. Do not give
out half-hearted squalls. Do not *try* to focus your intent and spirit into
your technique and shout, do so.

There may be times, however, when the use of a fully verbal shout
is self-defeating, such as when the silent removal of an opponent is
called for. When you expel the air from the diaphragm, open your
mouth as though yelling but do not make a sound. Give the shout
mentally. The ferocity of your technique is concentrated in the exhalation of air and the silent, mental shout. This may be a bit more difficult to master, but it is of equal importance to the training system.

Illusions

The modern warrior must seek more than the physical perfection
of his trade. There must also be an ideal and a code to motivate and
guide the warrior's potential for destruction, as well as to help him
see through the traps and webs laid for him by those not of the warrior way, who would seek to use that power. These beliefs that are
grouped together in a code must be deeply ingrained, beliefs of the
spirit rather than just the intellect. A warrior accepts the world as it
is, not as someone else wants him to see it, or as he wishes it were,
and accepts it in the beauty and savagery of reality. Then when he
sees truth, he may act upon it as he sees fit to do so. In this manner
one has a positive effect on destiny and will achieve tangible results
in life. Knowing that the cause for which you strive is just or right,
keeping beliefs that you hold true in mind, will allow you to act in accordance with your way at all times, and you will never be wrong in
deed or speech.

The first thing to consider is that you, as a human being, have the right to happiness as a birthright. You have the right not be be hurt physically or mentally. You have the right to pursue happiness in your own fashion, so long as it does not infringe on the right of others to be happy, or harm others. In other words, you have the moral imperative to defend yourself and your kin from aggression. If you choose to allow aggression against you to go unchallenged ("going with the flow" is one saying), you fail your birthright. Indeed, you also allow the aggressor to continue on his ill-conceived course until finally someone else must stop him. This is not to say that you should meet every act of aggression, such as a loud or pushy person, with violence. Simply stand up to them, keeping the same calm attitude that you should maintain in combat. If they choose violence, counter it. There are many methods of turning aside hostility. Violence is the last resort. You do have the RIGHT to defend yourself, though.

The basis for a warrior's philosophy must use ideals such as truth, courage, honor, and loyalty, to guide the training as well as the life of a warrior. Justice becomes an extension of this concept. On the other hand, certain negative emotions and thought patterns must be dealt with, so that the webs of illusion are lessened and you are no longer controlled by them.

Four Sicknesses

The ancient Japanese Samurai thought of four particular emotions as sicknesses which led to all forms of failure in life. They are Worry, Fear, Doubt, and Surprise. They are essentially self-manufactured illusions and may be controlled through proper training, but the main lesson to be learned from martial training is to utilize the strategies of fighting in one's everyday life. To overcome the illusions that are a product of our society, the way each of us are raised, the many small burdens we have borne through life require almost tunnel vision on the purpose of training itself.

Worry — If you are concerned with one particular aspect of your life when you are trying to perform in another area, you will be distracted from the singular goal that should be your motivation. In combat your singular goal is to successfully accomplish your mission; in self-defense your goal is to fend off and defeat your opponent. If, in these extreme situations you are thinking about or concerned with anything that is not directly related to what you are doing, you cannot have that vital tunnel vision. You cannot perform at full capacity.

The solution to worry is to learn to compartmentalize your daily affairs. When a situation arises, do what you can to resolve it. If it is not resolvable put it away into its own 'compartment' until such a time as you are directly faced with it again. Do not let it interfere with your other affairs or goals. An example of not doing this is the person that leaves work preoccupied with something that has happened there, and walks into traffic in front of an automobile. The warrior would be thinking about walking, observing the people around him, the flow of traffic, his mind clear of the past until he was able to reflect on it in an area he knew was secure for this purpose.

Fear — This includes what are called phobias as well; not simply the minor fears one encounters from day to day. For the warrior, fear is the most devastating of opponents, for it clouds the judgment and counsels flight when it is not in order. It can paralyze the mind and weaken the body. One cannot totally banish fear, or suppress it either. To do so is mentally unhealthy and leads to neurosis as the mind finds ways to vent the pressure. Post combat stress disorders are an example of this. So one finds ways to use the fear, channeling it into positive energy.

When you find yourself in a confrontation, stay calm and practice the deep breathing method. Observe your terrain, noting obstacles. Prepare yourself in this manner for anything that your potential opponent may offer. This channels the fear that may be rising in you into positive activities. If necessary, move into an open area where you will have room to fight. Remain calm but never let the opponent think he has you intimidated. Maintain a stern expression, a strong posture. If you speak to him, choose a tone and words that are neither threatening nor indicative of weakness. "Please don't hurt me", is not recommended; neither is "Get away ya punk, or I'll tear your heart out".

Once action begins, fight from a posture of strength, but not viciousness, which is often inspired by fear. Hatred, too, is often a product of fear. Such a feeling may overpower you and not the opponent. Fight from the sure knowledge that you are right in defending yourself with no other consideration. Beat the opponent because he is wrong, not out of hate or fear.

If you have an overwhelming fear of a certain thing, a phobia, this requires more than rechanneling to live with. Fear is a natural reaction to what your outer senses perceive as a threat, which may be dealt with when you understand that because of your training you cannot be threatened. Phobias are fear of something that your inner mind has come to recognize as an ultimate threat; whether it is truly a threat or not is immaterial, since your mind recognizes it as one. An irrational fear of heights for a paratrooper is deadly; a panic when faced with a knife is the end of a street encounter. The more that your mind fears a particular encounter, whether it is fear of being hit or cut or falling from a high place, the more panic will ensue when you meet a similar situation in real life. Since the tasks a warrior may encounter, even in a benevolent situation, are myriad, phobias must be dealt with.

When you meditate, envision yourself confronted by an opponent armed with a knife or having to climb to a high place to accomplish a strongly desired goal. Envision ways in which to overcome the problems as you meditate. See yourself actively overcoming your problem. At first you may see yourself fall or be killed by the knife, but slowly you will find ways to win, to take the knife away or turn it against the opponent; you will reach the pinnacle of the high place and survey the world below. Gradually you will win against the phobia, too. As your fighting skill improves, so too will your mastery over fear.

Doubt — A warrior must have great faith in his native ability, his skills, and weapons to be able to perform fully in combat. For the empty hand fighter, the weapons are the hands and the feet, the body and mind. More than that, the weapons are the techniques themselves and the ability to deliver them with effect. The only sure way to overcome doubt, which erodes the spirit and skill of a fighter, is to train incessantly in his skills and hone them to perfection. This applies to all aspects of life. The lawyer must know that his courtroom skill is the best that he can make it, through long hours of research and study. When you *know* something with your subconscious as well as your conscious intellect, it has become a part of you. You and your weapons are in unity, and you need not think before you react if you are attacked.

The methods put forth in this manual are battle tested in both the arena of war and on the streets in self-defense. When internalized they will serve faithfully for defense. The training methods may seem repetitious, but they work to ingrain the fighting skills into the warrior with a discipline that will not be broken under any stress once they are internalized. When you train, look for the effectiveness of your technique. Question it. If you find it sound, learn to rely on it; believe in it. Practice it until you are sure that you have mastered it. In this way doubt will never assail you.

Surprise — When you are assailed suddenly and without warning you are at a disadvantage. Whether it is physical or mental, surprise has always been considered an advantage by persons looking for an easy opening in their opponent's defense. For a warrior it could mean instant death or serious injury. At the least, it psychologically off balances you, causing mistakes.

To guard against it, you must keep your mind on what you are doing as you do it. Be aware of what is around you. Do not let your mind wander or become preoccupied with other matters.

Here are some simple examples of personal security that keep you from being surprised in any form. When you turn a corner, take it very wide so that you can see what is coming toward you from the opposite direction. When you seat yourself do not trap yourself under a table by pulling your chair in tightly under it. Do not seat yourself deeply in couches or overstuffed chairs so that you cannot rise quickly if needed. Do not walk through crowds, skirt them when possible. When entering a door, open it and pause for a second, step partially in and observe the area with your peripheral vision. In other words, pay attention to your surroundings and to how you interact with those surroundings. This is not paranoia, but simple self-preservation and alertness. Try to do these things without drawing attention to yourself for that often provokes others as well. Make these things a habit, not something you do one day and forget the next.

Being prepared is another form of negating surprise. If you have done all that you can to prepare yourself, it is hard for an opponent to take you by surprise. In business, if you have all of the pertinent facts and papers at hand, you are prepared to do business and cannot be taken unaware by a competitor. The same is true for the warrior. This covers all aspects of life. It often entails some research on your part, but that is rewarded when you not only survive the encounter, but come through unscathed as well. In combat this is essential. You must have the proper intelligence, and have assimilated it, interpreted it correctly, then understood it before you can act on it with proper preparation. If you know that you are going into a bad area, you can prepare yourself for that. If you think that you are being set up you can devise a method of turning the tables. But observation, research, and alertness all come first. Make this a part of your life just as you do the fighting methods.

The Webs

Others often seek to bind the warrior with words when they cannot do so by other means; words that strike various response centers in those of the warrior's spirit. These are the webs of deceit, woven by others, not things which arise from within a warrior such as the Four Sicknesses. Often the web is conditioned into us from our earliest years; a conditioning that is hard to fight.

To overcome this conditioning, one must begin by accepting the world as it is now. Religious philosophies aside, the world is a violent place full of both good and evil in varying degrees, often coexisting side-by-side. It is beautiful and savage at the same time. Things are not often "as they should be" nor as we might want them to be. Ideals should not be viewed as how things might be, but how things really are and how we could change them to be. This is the warrior's motivation; to have a positive effect on destiny to bring the wrongs of the world into line with a certain idealism. Action in the pursuit of these goals is what the warrior strives for intuitively. If the world were the Utopia it might be, then warriors might not be needed; but the world is not and warriors are needed.

Loyalty — The concept of loyalty is often abused by those who have control over the actions of others. Loyalty for a warrior should be to his comrades, his kin, his leaders and nation. But the greatest loyalty for a warrior should be to his ideals. If the nation or his leaders ask something of him that is beyond the range of the warrior's personal code of right and wrong, he is correct to refuse such an order. Further, he would be correct to work to correct the wrong, no matter the price to himself. As has happened too often throughout man's history, warriors have been betrayed by their leaders, and by their civilians when the warriors did not follow their own ideals but the words of men. Weigh such things carefully before committing yourself to action. Fair words often harbor dark designs.

Loyalty to others does not require you to do their bidding, nor to be their slave. It means simply that you are their comrade through thick and thin, that you stand together no matter what popular opinion is; that you can rely on one another, despite the words of men.

Mercy — This is an ideal that is often used to weaken the ideals of a warrior. Mercy from the strong is natural. When a person is sure of his own abilities he has no need to prove himself to others, and he may show others mercy. This means to help the weak, the victims. When you are offered violence, this does not mean that you should concern yourself with the problems of the opponent. If he had a terrible childhood, if he is poor, these things are not your concern after he has attacked. The mental or economic straits of others are not your concern when they clearly show themselves to be your adversary.

In combat, when you are fighting an enemy force, there is no time for considering mercy either. After you have beaten them totally, mind and body, then is the time to consider how to treat them. Do not regard their losses during the heat of battle; if by heavy losses to the enemy you ensure your own nation or family peace for years to come, you are justified.

One should show mercy to those that deserve it, starting with your own circle of kin or battle group, and if there is some left to go around after that, to your opponents. While your own need help, do not be concerned with the rest of the world. However, there is never a reason to be unnecessarily harsh or cruel.

Duty — Do not confuse duty with what others expect of you, for the two are utterly different. Duty is a debt you owe yourself to fulfill obligations and matters of honor that you have assumed voluntarily. Paying that debt can entail anything from years of patient work to an instant willingness to sacrifice your life. It may be difficult, but the reward is self-respect, and knowing that you have been true to your ideals.

But there is no reward for doing what others expect of you, just because it is expected. It is easier to deal with an assailant than it is with the psychological vampires who want "just a moment of your time please . . . it won't take very long". Time is the total capital of your life and the minutes are painfully few, so those who seek to waste your time are actually stealing it from you. By simply saying NO you will not be burdened with that type of parasitism. However, this by no means suggests that you can or should not help a comrade, or even a stranger. Just do not let them become a burden around your neck. While it may be your duty to give a comrade a hand, it is not your duty to carry him on your back the rest of your life. Let the choice of action be yours and not what any group or individual seems to think is right. If a group or individual is right, sometimes a deluge of opinions tends to push one away from that truth, so thought must be given to this.

Honor — For the person that wishes to become a warrior, to walk the often solitary path, the decision must be based on a belief that there is no other way of life worth living, including the ethos that goes with it. This becomes a pact you make with yourself. Part of this ethos is the concept of personal honor, something that is intangible, one of the webs woven by those around us at times, but also something that we must have ourselves. You must work out your own honor system for yourself. For the warrior it becomes a code, a way of life, unbending and unaltered, often without any verbal guidelines. When all of your possessions are far from you, you will still have your honor, your core.

A handshake or simply saying, "I will do this", is your bond, more concrete than any signature on paper should be. Your actions demonstrate your code. To abuse your knowledge, betray a comrade, lie, things such as that, you will have broken your pact with yourself and have lost your honor. If you act in accordance with your beliefs as well as you can, you will retain your honor always.

When you are able to deal with yourself and the illusions others try to bind you with, you will be an effective warrior. Much of this can only be learned by doing and experiencing, and not from reading; but these few passages may give you food for thought. The seed must die so that the plant may grow.

PART TWO

Chapter Five

The Path

Methods

The techniques of fighting are varied to meet the demands of actual combat, which moves and flows with a rhythm all its own. The techniques are taught in a graduated method in order of importance to the fighter, and difficulty in mastery of them. It is generally considered to be harder to master the correct methods of striking than the correct methods of blocking.

Before you may perform any of these with power you must first learn to stand, walk, turn, and move in such a manner as to permit yourself to instantly lunge forward in attack, or fall back in defense, in any direction. Stances and stepping methods are the first steps along the path of total fighting skills.

Stances: Walking the Mountain

Stances in the martial arts are the basis for power transference, the technique of body movement that makes the martial art techniques so devastating. If the feet are not placed correctly, the weight held too far back or forward, the impact of the blow you are attacking with will push you backward; if the body does not pivot from the hips you will be utilizing only the strength of the limb and not the entire body. In boxing this is called an arm punch and is not considered effective. In martial arts it is considered a waste of time. If you are not properly balanced and you take a blow you may go down. On the other hand, when you are properly tucked into a stance the chances of going down from a blow are much less, and the effect of your blows will be enhanced.

Stances used for fighting are shorter and narrower than one would find in a traditional system. This is for the mobility that they provide in combat. If you desire more stability, increase the width of your stance, making it "deeper". When you are training in static forms train your stances to be deep and wide: solid. This strengthens your thighs, knees, and ankles so that if you ever have to use these stances in life or death combat and shorten them again, you will be able to move with twice the speed you normally have in the deep stances.

Stances for combat are not static. Do not lock yourself into one

stance and surrender your option of mobility in a fight. They are transitory by concept, encompassing nearly the full range of human movement as applicable to combative concepts. Some aspects of training
use static, unmoving stances, but it is only to build the strength of
the individual stance, not to train you to assume one position and
freeze there. During the execution of many block-counterstrike combinations you may pass through two or three stances quickly. Also,
do not use the stances to pose for your opponent. Do nothing to alert
him (them) to the fact that you are a trained and skilled fighter until
they commit themselves against you. Then let your actions speak of
your fighting prowess, not your posture. Equally, do not be intimidated
if an opponent assumes exotic stance. Surprise is one of your secret
weapons, do not surrender it lightly.

Stepping

Glide Step — This is the basic method of stepping in combat. From
the Ready stance (feet shoulder-width apart, feet parallel) bring the
left foot to the right foot, raising the heel from the floor first, then the
ball. Move it in a semicircular motion to the left front. The foot should
be just slightly off the floor during the step, but not touching it
anywhere. When you replace the foot on the floor, put the ball of the
foot down first, being sure of your footing, then lower the heel. Bend
the knee of the supporting (right) leg during the step for balance and
greater support. Bring the right foot to the left in a semicircular movement. Do not pause when the feet become parallel, but bring the right
foot to your right front, ball touching down first and then the heel.
This is the advancing movement.

Retreating is essentially the same. With the right foot forward, bring
it back to the left foot in the same semicircular motion, then to the
right rear. Set the ball of the foot down first, then the heel. Bring the
left foot to the right foot, then back to the left forming a Ready stance.

Turning with the Glide step is also the same. From the Ready
stance, look to your straight right. Raise the heel of the right foot,
pivot on the ball of the left foot, bring the right foot in close to the
left foot as you pivot and step out to your right in the stance of your
choice.

Return to the Ready stance, then step the left foot to your left front.
Turning to the rear is essentially the same as turning to the side. Look
over your right shoulder, then bring your right foot to your left in the
same semicircular motion. Pivot on the ball of the left foot and step
to the straight rear with your right foot.

Drag Step — The Drag step is used for more controlled movement in combat where you are moving in a confined area and are in close proximity to the opponent. It provides good support for you if you are struck while moving, the dragging leg giving you something to brace yourself with if you fall back, and it provides excellent forward thrust when you choose to close the gap with the opponent.

From a Ready stance use the Glide step to shift the right foot forward. Raise the heel of the left foot and drag it on the inner edge, just below the big toe, to the heel of the right foot. The dragging action is in a straight line, not a semicircle. When you step forward with the right foot again, use the Glide step motion, then drag the left foot forward again. When you step forward, the distance is usually not greater than a twelve inch step. When you drag the rear foot forward, form a stance with it, so that the actual drag does not cover very much ground.

To retreat lift the rear foot and set it back twelve inches. Then move the front foot onto its ball and drag it back, perhaps half the distance of the step, and form a stance. Keep both legs bent during the entire movement, using the rear leg to thrust forward from during the step forward; thrust backward with the front leg during retreat.

Turning follows the same procedures as for the Glide step.

Foot Replacement — From a Ready stance use the Glide step to move your right foot forward. Pick up the heel of the left foot, and slide it forward on the ball of the foot parallel to the right foot, but not touching it. Set the heel of the left foot down and step the right foot forward using the Glide step method. This is a rapid movement for closing the gap with the opponent. It is used so that he does not know until you are in motion with the next step which side you are attacking with.

To retreat using this method pick up the forward foot and move it in the Glide step to the rear foot. Then step backward with the front foot.

Turning is the same as for the Glide step.

Cross Step — This is used mostly when in a stance where the feet are parallel and you are facing the side (the straddle stance, for example), but it may be used in a forward stance or for angular movement. In a Ready stance turn to look to your straight right, moving only your head. Pick up the left foot and cross it behind the right foot at the ankle, resting the ball of the left foot on the ground close to the sword foot edge of the right foot. Pick up the right foot and lift it over the left foot, placing it to the straight right and forming another Ready stance with both feet flat on the ground.

Retreating is the same, but in reverse. Turn to face the left. Cross your right foot behind your left, then step over the right with the left foot, forming a Ready stance.

There is no turning for this stepping method.

Stances

Ready Stance — The Ready stance is the basic stance of the system. Stand with your feet together, shoulder width apart, toes pointing forward. Keep the torso and head erect, hands hanging at the sides open and relaxed. In this system, this is the stance from which all action starts.

Natural Right Front Stance — This is often used as a preparatory stance just before combat is joined. From the Ready stance use the Glide step to move the right foot forward. The feet should be shoulder width apart, front foot pointed toward the opponent, rear foot turned at a forty-five degree angle to the left, away from the lead foot. The knees are slightly bent, and the feet should be twelve to fifteen inches apart from the heel of the lead foot to the toes of the rear foot. The hands may be crossed at the chest or at the sides in a relaxed stance.

Natural Left Front Stance — This is the exact opposite of the Natural Right Front Stance, but with the left foot forward. Everything else is the same.

Fighting Stance — This is the basic fighting posture of the system, used mostly before the combat moves to close range. It is an effective guarding posture and provides good maneuverability. Stances are named for either the leg that is forward if the weight is evenly distributed, or the weight-bearing leg. The Fighting stance is named for the lead leg. From a Ready stance, use the Glide step to move the right leg forward about twenty inches to the right front. The feet should be a little more than shoulder width apart. The toes of the lead foot are pointing straight ahead at the opponent; the knee of the lead leg is bent. The rear foot is turned forty-five degrees away from the lead foot and is kept flat on the floor; the rear leg is bent at the knee. The weight is evenly distributed on both legs. Turn your torso slightly to the left so that you are not squarely facing the opponent.

Front Stance — This is a forward lunging stance that creates great momentum as you shift into it. From a Ready stance use a Glide step method to bring the left foot to the left front. As you step, straighten the right leg forcefully, pushing with it. The left foot is pointing straight ahead, and the knee is bent. The rear foot is turned away from the lead foot at a forty-five degree angle and the knee is locked straight. The torso is turned square to the opponent. Keep both feet flat on the floor. The weight is distributed with about seventy percent on the

Ready stance

Front Stance   Front view — Hands in mid level guard
He is executing lead thrust punch.

He is blocking lunge punch and attacking with spear hand to eye.

front leg, thirty percent on the rear leg. It is named for the weight-bearing leg, the lead leg.

Back Stance — This is often used as a fading, retreating movement, falling back away from the opponent's attack until you can block and counter. From a Ready stance use the glide step method to bring the right foot forward to the right front. The lead foot points straight at the opponent and the lead knee is bent slightly. The rear foot is turned ninety degrees away from the lead foot and the rear leg knee is bent. The heels are less than a shoulder width apart in this stance, making it much narrower than any of the other stances. It is about twenty inches deep from heel to heel. Seventy percent of the weight is on the rear leg, thirty percent is on the front leg. It is named for the weight-bearing leg, the rear leg. Turn the torso slightly to the left as in the Fighting stance.

Straddle Stance — This is a side fighting stance and is often seen as a prime fighting stance. However, it is easier to shift into this stance when an opponent attacks from the side. From the Ready stance pick up the left foot and step straight forward pivoting on the ball of the right foot, so that you face the straight right. Bend the knees of both legs with the feet a little more than shoulder width apart and the heels in a straight line. The toes of both feet are pointed to the straight right. Turn your head to look over your left shoulder to what is now your straight left. This stance is named for the direction that you are facing; in this case it would be a left Straddle stance. Moving forward or backward from this stance is generally accomplished using the Cross step method.

Angular Stance — From the Ready stance, step your right foot to your front right using the Glide step. Now, pivoting on the ball of the right foot, slide the left foot back so that the heel is on the straight back line. You should be in a Straddle stance, but turned at an angle to the straight forward line. This is often used in slipping an attack or in preparing for an angular attack once your opponent has attacked along your center line. Your torso is turned slightly to the left so that you do not face your opponent squarely; both knees are bent as in the Straddle stance.

Back Stance
Front view

Straddle stance with hands in mid level guard

Straddle stance with hands in mid level guard

Chart

To understand the accompanying chart, the arrow is pointing at the opponent and is the direction you are facing in the stance. The black dot is where the majority of weight is concentrated in the stance. The X where the lines cross is the center of your body as you take the stance.

Stances

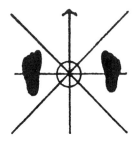

Ready Stance

Natural Right Front Stance

Natural Left Front Stance

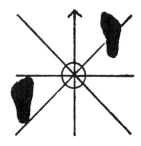

Fighting Stance

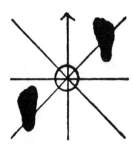

Front Stance

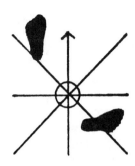

Back Stance

Straddle Stance

**Angular Stance from
the Natural Front Stance**

Training Methods

Static training means that you hold one stance for a period of time, allowing your body to become used to that position, then shift into another stance. This is called Walking the Mountain.

Begin in the Ready stance. Step forward into a right Fighting stance, as wide and deep as you can, and settle into it. Stay in this position for three minutes. Now, using the Glide step, step forward into a left Fighting stance and hold it for three minutes. Shift into a left Front stance by sliding the left foot forward and snapping the rear leg straight. Hold it for three minutes. Step forward into a right Front stance and hold it for three minutes. Shift into a left Back stance by turning the left foot out ninety degrees and shifting the weight backward onto the left leg and hold it for three minutes. Return to the Ready stance.

Perform this exercise until you do not feel any strain in the three minute time period for any stance. When you can hold every stance in the above exercise for three minutes comfortably, begin the next exercise.

Start in the Ready stance. Use the Glide step to form a right Fighting stance and hold it for three minutes. Advance with the left foot into a left Fighting stance. Hold it for three minutes, then lunge forward by straightening the rear leg and pushing strongly forward into a left Front stance, holding it for three minutes. Step back into a left Back stance and hold it for three minutes, then lunge forward into a right Front stance and hold it for three minutes. Return to a Ready stance by stepping back; hold it briefly. Then step the left foot straight left and form a left Straddle stance, holding for three minutes. Step the right foot to your right front and form an Angular stance, holding it for three minutes. Bring the right foot back and form a right Straddle stance and hold it for three minutes, then step the left foot to your front and form an Angular stance, holding for three minutes. Return to the Ready stance.

When you are able to perform this exercise with ease, add more time to each stance.

Linear Movement Concepts

Static training strengthens the individual stance, but does not train you in how to move in fighting. There are essentially two methods of offense-defense: linear movement which is straight line, and angular which is lateral or at an angle to the opponent. Linear movement is the most basic. When performing these exercises keep your hands in the mid level guard.

Begin in a Ready stance. Use the Glide step to form a right Fighting stance, then step forward with the left foot to form a left Fighting stance. Now, retreat by stepping backward with the left foot to form a right Fighting stance. Retreat again by stepping backward with the right foot to form a left Fighting stance. You should be at your original starting position; return to the Ready stance.

Now step forward with the right foot forming a left Back stance. Without stepping, shift into a right Front stance. Step forward with the left foot and form a right Back stance, then shift without stepping into a left Front stance. Retreat by stepping backward with the left foot forming a left Back stance, then shift into a right Front stance. Step backward with the right foot forming a right Back stance, then shift into a left Front stance. Return to the Ready stance. This exercise is to teach the idea of body shifting in attack and defense. When you step forward into the Back stance you are blocking, stepping into and inside an attack, then shifting forward into a Front stance for attack. When you are retreating into a Back stance you are fading back from his attack, then shifting forward into a Front stance for your counterattack. Use the Glide step for this exercise.

From the Ready stance bring the right foot forward, pivoting on the ball of the left foot, and form a right Straddle stance. Use the cross step method and advance three steps forward. Maintain your right Straddle stance. Turn to look to the left and use the cross step method to return to the starting point, maintaining a left Straddle stance as you step.

This is the basic concept of linear movement. You may mix the stances after you have performed the basic routine, trying for more speed of movement and positioning as you do so, but do not allow your movements to become sloppy.

Angular Movement Concepts

Angular movement is a slightly more advanced fighting skill and requires more training in the method and timing of the opponent to be used successfully. It is more effective when you are able to use it because it puts you outside of your opponent's ability to effectively attack you, while you may attack him cleanly. Keep the angles of movement in mind when performing these exercises.

Begin in a Ready stance. Use the Glide step and step the right foot to your right front forming an Angular stance. Step the left foot to your right rear and form a right Straddle stance. Then shift into a right Front stance by advancing the right foot forward and straightening the left leg with a snap. You have side-stepped the opponent's attack with the Angular stance, further flanking him with the Straddle stance and then counterattacking with the Front stance.

Return to the starting point in a Ready stance. Step the left foot to your left front forming an Angular stance. Then shift into a left Front stance by thrusting the right leg straight and the right hip forward. Turn the left toes forward. Shift into a front facing Straddle stance by shifting the hips to your right strongly and turning the toes of both feet to face your straight right. (In this stance, it would be straight forward.) You have just side-stepped your opponent's attack, counterattacked when you shifted into the Front stance, then finished him off with the shift into the Straddle stance with a left hand blow. This teaches body shifting with technique, one technique winding the body up for the next as you move around your opponent.

You will find more uses for angular movement than for linear, but to be learned fully it must be practiced with a training partner. As he commits himself to the attack, you must learn to move. Before he can recover and shift positions, you must have hit or thrown him. When you begin using the striking methods in training, add these drills to the empty-hand training methods, as well as others that will spring up from this concept of movement. When you fully understand the basic concept the variations will come to you naturally; when you fully understand any one principle you'll know a hundred techniques.

Striking Methods — The Body As A Weapon
Hand Techniques

The basic weapon of a fighter is the focused hand strike, and with good reason. The kicking techniques are stronger, but are more difficult to learn and perfect. Also, if your opponent can get over or around your kick and close to you, and you are not able to deliver strong and focused hand strikes to him, you are at his mercy. The object of training is to develop each technique to perfection so that in combat when you see or create an opening, you land one strong blow to the open vital striking point and end the fight. Often, of course, it is necessary to attack with a combination of techniques because of the fluidity of a real fight; one may not land as planned, or the opponent may move at the last second, not absorbing the full impact of the blow, making follow-up techniques necessary. Each technique in a combination should be potentially devastating. However, do not throw one just for the sake of filling the air between you without speed, focus, or power.

It is relevant to consider the potential of a properly focused hand strike. A middle-aged, one hundred forty pound Japanese man recorded an impact of over two thousand foot pounds on an Impactometer at Long Island State University some years ago with one punch. This is not beyond the capability of anyone that practices their technique faithfully. Two thousand foot pounds of force is more than enough to end most fights.

Hand techniques are divided into two categories: the straight thrust which moves in a straight line from your body to the opponent's, and the strike which moves in an arc from your body to the opponent's.

Straight Thrust — The shortest distance between two objects is a straight line. With this in mind, the straight thrusting techniques are often the fastest and strongest methods of hitting the opponent. From the point of the five points of attack, the straight thrust covers the straight forward point. Strikes cover the other four. The basic thrust is the closed fist punch.

Straight Punch — In the Ready stance, extend the right hand, still open, out at shoulder level. Bend the fingers into the palm at the middle knuckles, pulling them tight. Then fold the bent fingers into the palm and pull them tight, making a fist. Fold the thumb over the first two fingers between the first and second joints, keeping it down and out of the way. This is the proper formation of the fist and it is always made in the same way and kept tight. Never try to punch or strike with a fist in any way if you have not tightened it first.

Retract the hand that has been formed into a fist and place both hands in the mid level guard, either hand in the lead. For this description, place the right hand in the reverse position, formed into a fist, the left hand extended and open in the lead position. Rotate your right hip forward with a sharp snap, extend your right shoulder forward, thrust your arm forward, and aim at a point on your own center line about chest height. This is the basic thrust punch, and the movement is done in the order listed, though when done at full speed the acceleration is barely noticeable.

There are two types of punches in martial arts, the corkscrew or traditional style and the vertical fist punch in which the fist is not turned palm downward upon impact. The corkscrew punch leaves the chamber (guard position) with the palm facing the opposite arm, and as it approaches its target it rotates so that the palm is facing downward, locking the wrist at the moment of impact. There are various reasons that this punch is too slow and has a greater chance of being jammed before the full rotation is completed. For these reasons, the vertical fist punch is often the best for combative use.

That is what is described here.

Form a right Fighting stance with hands in the mid level guard. Pick a point on your own center line and snap your hip, then shoulder, then arm forward toward that point. Keep your punching elbow (the left arm in this case) in close to your side. Do not let it bend outward turning this into a circular punch. Also, do not let your arm extend all the way. Focus so that your arm is still slightly bent at the elbow when you complete the punch. If you practice punching with the arm snapping straight at each repetition you may damage your elbow. Also, you will not be getting the full power of your punch into your target when you begin heavy bag training. You will be "surface punching" the target. Leave the fist with the palm facing to your right. At the moment of impact, or focus, lower the forefist slightly so that you are striking with the front of the first two foreknuckles only, not the two bottom knuckles of the fist or the four knuckles. This provides maximum penetration for the punch. Do not lean forward into this technique. Keep your feet flat, knees bent, and your back straight. Boxers come up on the ball of the foot to generate more power, but power is generated through the use of acceleration, keeping your feet flat, directly connecting yourself with the ground, linking your entire body through tension and stance with the earth. This is how one slight man can produce over two thousand foot pounds of force with one punch. As you deliver the left punch, rotate the right hip and arm sharply to the right rear as a counterbalance for the force being created with the left arm. Return the arm quickly to the guard position.

There are three methods of punching with a straight punch.

Reverse Punch — The reverse punch is done from whichever side is back in a stance, in the way described above. It is often used as a counterpunch and is considered the strongest of the three punching methods.

Lead Punch — The lead punch is done from whichever side is forward in a stance with the same body mechanics as the reverse punch. Assume a left Fighting stance with the hands in the mid level guard, lead hand formed into a fist. Rotate the left hip forward strongly, then the left shoulder, and the left arm while snapping the right side to the right rear. Punch to your own center line. In a Fighting stance you are turned slightly to the right when you begin the punch. When you complete a lead punch you should be turned so that only your left side faces the opponent; the left arm should not be locked out straight, but slightly bent at the elbow. This is not a boxing "jab", but a one-punch knockout blow. As soon as you have completed the punch return your hand to the guard position. Do not leave it dan-

Lead Punch
(1) Back stance

(2) Shift into fighting stance, begin punch

(3) Finish punch

gling out in the air.

Lunge Punch — From a Ready stance, using the Glide step, step forward with the right foot forming a right Fighting stance. Just as the foot sets down firmly on the heel, strike to your own center line with a right lead punch. As you step, cock the hips to the right for the punch, but do not turn your right shoulder or pull the right fist away from the guard position. Both of these movements will alert your opponent to your intention. Punch to your own center line and snap the left side to the left rear as you attack. Immediately return your hand to the guard position after the punch.

Combination — The basic three-punch combination is from a Fighting stance; for the sake of description it will be a left Fighting stance. Hold your hands in the mid level guard. Punch to your own center line with a right reverse punch, pulling your left lead side to the left rear. Tense for just a split second, and retreat the arm to the guard position. As you pull the right arm back, punch to your own center line with a left lead punch. Tense for a second, then, using the glide step, bring the right foot forward into a right Front stance, and punch with the right arm in a lunge punch. Training in this combination will give you a feel for the use of the body in combination attacks, especially where punches and strikes are mixed together, where one blow winds up the body for the next blow. This is vitally important for the understanding of thrusting.

Middle Single Knuckle Fist — This thrusting technique has greater penetration than the punch but is used more selectively until you have hardened your fist to the degree that it may be used on hard striking points. When you form your fist, do it in the same way as for a punch, but extend the middle knuckle of the second finger, the middle finger. Place the ball of the thumb on the first joint of the middle finger to reinforce it and tighten the ring and index fingers against the sides of it. It is delivered in the reverse, lead, and lunge punch methods. It is primarily used against the solar plexus, lower abdomen, and other soft targets; however, with training, it may be used against *any* target, any vital striking point on the body. It may also be used as a strike in the inverted fist and hook punch methods to the side of the neck and temple. Because of the penetration, it may be a killing blow. In the straight thrusting method it is used as a vertical fist thrust.

Straight Finger Thrust — This is also called a spear hand. The hand is left open with the fingers held straight, tensed and tightly together for strength. The thumb is tucked down close to the palm to protect it. This thrust also has great penetration and is generally used for soft target areas. When thrust into the throat or solar plexus

Lunge Punch — Reverse Punch Combination
(1) Fighting stance.

(2) Step forward into lunge punch

(3) Attack with reverse punch

the hand is held vertically; when used for the eyes it is held with the palm down horizontally. It is used in the reverse, lead, and lunge methods of the straight thrust method. Because of the penetration this thrust is capable of, it may be a killing blow. The tips of the four fingers are the striking points.

Palm Fist Thrust — This is an open hand method that does not penetrate but is capable of tremendous force, thrusting shock waves into the target area. Open the hand and cock the wrist back as far as it will go, exposing the heel of the palm as the striking point. The fingers are bent, clawed slightly to add tension to the palm and the thumb is held out away from the palm, also bent. The palm fist thrust may be used in the lead, reverse, or lunge methods of striking. There are three methods of holding the hand for this thrust. When striking into the abdomen or mid level, the hand is turned sideways so that the fingers are to the side (i.e. when striking the abdomen with a right palm fist the fingers are turned to the right). When attacking the high level the fingers are turned up. When attacking the bladder the fingers are turned down, the palm upward slightly. The palm fist, like the middle single knuckle fist, may also be used as a strike such as an uppercut or hook, with equal effect. It will not harm the hand if the wrist is kept tense at the moment of impact.

Strikes — The strike is like a rock on the end of a whip which uncoils its power in an arcing motion, then snaps at the last moment and recoils for the next strike. They do not usually penetrate the opponent's body as do straight thrusts, but rather send shock waves inward, compressing organs or shattering bones and forcing them inward. Strikes are not as fast as thrusts but are more deceptive, often coming in from blind angles so that the opponent is not able to prepare for them or guard against them.

Hook Punch — The fist is formed in the same manner as for a straight punch. It may be done as a lead, reverse, or lunge technique, but the footwork is slightly different for a hook punch. Form a right Fighting stance with the hands in the mid level guard. Pick up the heel of the right foot and cock the hips to the right in preparation for the punch. Simultaneously, pivot on the ball of the right foot to the right and rotate the right hip strongly to the front. From the lead hand position of the mid level guard, clench the lead hand into a fist and rotate the shoulder forward. Your target is your own center line. Slam the right heel down to the right as though stamping on a bug as you strike to your own center line with an arcing motion of the right fist, turning the fist so that the palm faces downward just before impact. You are almost in an Angular stance at the completion of the hook.

Straight thrust

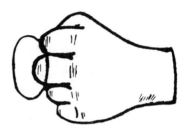

Middle single knuckle fist

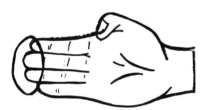

Spear hand

Palm fist

Rising Palm Fist Strike
(1) Begin in fighting stance

(2) He attacks with reverse punch. Block should be outer parry

(3) Attack chin with palm fist

The striking point is the same as in a straight punch, the front of the two foreknuckles. Tense the wrist just before impact, and tense the entire body at impact. This strike may be done to any of the vital striking points equally. The stepping method is called the Drop Step and is employed in many strikes in one form or another to add momentum to the strike. The turn-stomp motion must be done in accompaniment with the hip rotation to enhance the acceleration; if they are done one behind the other you will lose time, slowing the strike rather than enhancing it. It cannot be done in reverse.

Inverted Fist Strike — This is also a closed fist technique. The fist is formed in the same manner as the straight punch fist. It may be done as a reverse, lead, or lunge technique, and the striking area is the same: the front of the two foreknuckles. In a right Fighting stance with the hands in the mid level guard, lower the left hand and turn the fist palm up, pulling to your left hip. Cock your hips to the left. When you thrust forward, come up slightly, aiming for the solar plexus. Rotate your hip forward as though you were scooping with a large shovel, thrusting with your left leg. The strike does not travel far beyond your own body. The elbow should not travel more than six inches past your hip. It is a close range, driving blow. In the lead and lunge versions, lower the lead hand and turn the palm of the fist upward. Cock your hips to the lead side, and thrust upward with the strike, with the same scooping motion of the hips. The upward penetration of the two foreknuckles to the throat, jaw, or solar plexus may be killing strikes.

Backfist — The fist is formed in the same way the straight punch fist is formed, but the striking area is the back of the two foreknuckles. It is usually delivered either as a lead or lunge technique, not from the reverse position. There are three methods of delivery, as follow.

(1) Across the Body — Form a right Fighting stance with the hands in the mid level guard. Cock the hips to the left and pull the right hand, closed into a fist, to the left shoulder, leaving the left hand in the standard position for the mid level guard. Snap your hips to the right then the right shoulder, then the right arm in a whipping motion, keeping the arm bent and cocked until the elbow reaches your own center line. Then drive the forearm and backfist into the strike, stopping at your own center line. Tense your wrist as the forearm whips out. The palm should be facing the left in an across the body strike. Use proper focus and tension. This, the across the body method of delivery, is potentially the strongest striking method. Use good hip rotation.

(2) Overhead Strike — From a left Fighting stance with the hands in the mid level guard, raise the left arm and cock it beside your head,

Across the Body Backfist
(1) Fighting stance.

(2) Defender uses mid level inner deflection block, chambers forearm for across the body back fist

(3) Strike

the fist near your left ear, palm facing back and down. Cock the hips to the left. Snap the hips forward and twist the torso to the right and downward in a slight spiraling motion. Begin the strike with the left shoulder, then the arm, snapping the forearm and backfist downward to your own center line. This may also be done with the reverse side. It is used mainly to strike the face and not the top of the head.

(3) Outside Strike — From a left Fighting stance with the hands in the mid level guard, pull the left arm out to the left, the fist cocked near your left ear with the palm facing straight forward and the left elbow straight out to your left. Cock your hips to the left. Snap them to the right quickly, then snap your left arm inward to your own center line. As your arm moves inward, rotate the fist so that the palm faces you as it reaches your center line, cocked outward slightly so that the backfist is extended. This is used to strike the side of the opponent's nose or his eye in a raking attack.

Bottom Fist Strike — The fist is formed in the same way that the straight punch is, but the striking area is the meaty portion of the bottom of the hand, and is also known as a hammer fist. There are three methods of delivery as follow, and may be used in the reverse, lead or lunge methods.

(1) Across the Body — This is the exact same as for the backfist strike except that the fist is turned palm down so that the bottom fist strikes the opponent. This is an excellent finishing technique since the bottom fist is hard to hurt.

(2) Overhead Strike — When this is applied in the lead or lunge method, raise the lead foot and thrust it down as you strike, adding to the momentum of the hip thrust and the downward swing of the arm. It is cocked and delivered the same way overhead backfist is, except that the fist is turned palm inward during the strike so that the bottom fist surface becomes the striking point. Never raise the arm straight up in the air in preparation for the strike; cock it as you did the backfist, fist beside the ear, elbow pointing out to the side.

(3) Outside Strike — This is the same as the backfist outside strike except that the fist is turned palm up at the moment of impact so that the bottom of the fist strikes. This is particularly effective against the side of the abdomen. Always strike to your own center line with proper hip rotation and tension.

Sword Hand Strike — This is an open hand strike that is performed in the same three methods as the backfist and bottom fist strikes. This strike may be performed in either the reverse, lead, or lunge methods. The striking surface is the meaty bottom edge of the hand between the little finger and the wrist bone, with the hand held open

Across the Body Sword Hand
(1) Start in fighting stance. Jam his lead leg with knee jam.

(2) Attack with sword hand.

Outer Sword Hand Strike
(1) Outer forearm block, chamber for strike

(2) Strike

much like the fingertip straight thrust, thumb tucked into the palm out of the way and the fingers held tightly together for support. It has great penetration and may be considered a killing blow to the front of the throat or the back of the neck.

Cupped Palm Strike — This is similar to the sword hand or the palm fist except the fingers are not held tightly together and are bent inward slightly rather than held straight or curled backward. This blow has only one application, to attack the ears with the cupped palms and force air into the passage there, rupturing the eardrums. From a Fighting stance with the hands in the mid level guard, form both hands into the cupped palm position. Bring them both out to a little more than shoulder width, then snap them forward and inward to your own center line, slapping your palms together in training to get the feel of the strike. In combat you may not be able to reach both ears. Strike with one hand in the cupped palm position to the ear and if this causes him to grimace, go for the other ear with the other hand. If it is possible to strike both ears simultaneously, do so.

Top Hand Strike — The hook punch is essentially a close range strike, with the target no further than eighteen inches away from you. There are times when you need a longer strike, arm's length for example, that moves in roughly the same line that the hook punch does. The top hand, or arc hand strike does this. Form the hand in the same method that the sword hand uses, pulling the thumb in close to the palm. The striking surface is the top of the hand between the first knuckle of the index finger and the thumb joint. It may be performed reverse, lead, or lunge, as may the hook punch. In a left Fighting stance with the hands in the mid level guard, cock the hips to the left and lower the left hand slightly, forming it into the top hand position. Snap the hips to the right, and use the drop step method, bringing the shoulder and upper arm to the right. Keep the left arm bent at the elbow at about a thirty degree angle to the upper arm. Strike to your own center line and use proper tension and focus. The reverse method is identical but the drop step is not used. This strike is ideal for the area just below the ears, side of the neck, jaw, and ribs. It may be used on any of the vital striking points and may be considered a killing blow if used on the front of the throat. It may also be used in an uppercut strike into the groin area at close range.

Top/Arc Hand Strike
(1) He attacks with lead punch. Block should be mid level palm fist parry

(2) Strike to temple with arc hand.

Training Methods

Begin by learning to execute each technique separately on a heavy punching bag. Hit the bag with full power, trying to drive the hand through the bag with focus, proper tension, and power. Get the feel of the hip rotation. Perform each technique on both sides equally so that you develop both your strong and weak sides together, neutralizing the concept of strong and weak sides. Perform ten of each technique on the bag at first, adding a few repetitions each week until you are able to perform thirty or more repetitions on the bag without pause. Your endurance for a real fight will be increased dramatically.

After you have a firm understanding of each individual technique, begin putting them together in combinations. Some examples are as follows:

(1) From a left Fighting stance with hands in the mid level guard, attack the high level of the bag with a left across the body backfist, followed immediately with a right straight punch to the mid level, then a left uppercut to the high level with a palm fist.

(2) From a right Fighting stance with the hands in the mid level guard, attack the high level with a right straight punch, cocking the left arm and executing a left outside sword hand also to the high level. Finish it off with a right high level vertical spear hand thrust.

(3) From a left Fighting stance with the hands in the mid level guard, attack with a high level left ridge hand, then follow up with a right straight punch to the mid level. Finish it with a left high level middle single knuckle fist.

This is by no means the extent of the possible combination attacks, but they should impart the general theory of combining hand striking and punching techniques for the maximum benefit in combat.

When you are able to create your own combinations fluidly, combine them with the stance training methods so that you are "shadow fighting". Move using the correct footwork, imagining an opponent in front of you, beside, or behind you, and respond to his attack appropriately with movement and hand technique. If you have a training partner, the two of you do this together. There is more in the last section which is strictly on training.

Inverted fist

Back Fist

Bottom fist

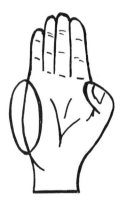

Sword hand

Top/Arc Hand

The Elbow

The importance of the elbow is often overlooked in martial arts, and wrongly so. It serves so many functions that it deserves a close look in any fighting art. In fighting, it serves three main functions: it provides snap and extension for hand strikes; it acts as a fulcrum for strong and rapid blocking; and it is devastating as a fighting weapon itself. In a stationary position such as the mid level guard, it makes excellent cover for the ribs and without much movement it can strike into kicks that attack your low level, injuring the opponent's leg.

Anatomically, the elbow is a moveable pivot point for the forearm which changes the extension of the arm. With just minor movement of the shoulder the elbow can be used to guard the body's flanks. During offensive movement the straightened elbow extends the fist when punching in a movement like a crankshaft and connecting rod during the compression, or power strike in an internal combustion engine, moving with much the same efficiency. The snap at the full extension of a punch comes from the tricep, the muscles of the back-arm, and the simultaneous relaxation of the bicep in the front of the arm. All of this is powered by the elbow's thrust.

While not one of the weakest joints, the elbows can easily be hurt. Elbow fractures can be caused by falling on the outstretched hand or on the joint itself. A severe blow to the joint can transmit force from bone to bone causing fracture or a splitting of the ends of the ulna, radius, or the humerus within the elbow area. Most often the actual breakage from a fall involves the area above or below the joint, a tribute to its natural strength; but a fall, a hard blow, a block, or especially a joint lock can dislocate the elbow. When this occurs, the bones in the forearm are often displaced. Other fall-related injury is a contusion or bone bruise which will show as swelling, discoloration and tenderness, all symptoms of a fracture or dislocation. A contusion will probably not involve an immediate loss of use of the forearm. The only way to be sure of the damage is an X-ray. Contusions can cause calcium deposits to form, hampering movement and irritating surrounding areas.

Strains and sprains result from forcing the elbow joint to hyperextension. For example, if an opponent snatches a relaxed hand and pulls hard he can cause a strain or sprain. The two are hard to differentiate since any elbow trauma involves both ligaments and tendons.

The elbow still makes an excellent short range weapon. The proper

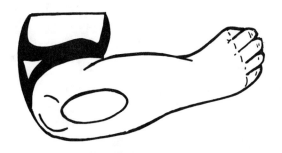

Lower elbow

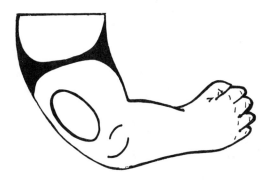

Upper elbow

striking points are the areas just above and below the point, and not the point itself. This helps prevent the possibility of shock waves being transmitted from the impact of the blow, as mentioned above, from bone to bone within the elbow joint. Elbow strikes are tactically and psychologically sound counterstrikes. Rather than having to block and step back, one can step in close after the block and attack with a single or a series of short, snapping blows with the elbows.

The mechanics of an elbow strike are based on the use of the hip, as in every technique, and in a twist of the torso more than in most other strikes. The upper arm guides the elbow to the target area rather than powering it. The arm should not travel far in a strike, since this strike is usually done at close range, and you have no time to wind up for a strong blow.

Begin in a right Fighting stance with the hands in the mid level guard. Snap the left hip forward quickly and strongly, turn the left shoulder into the movement, and snap your left elbow around in an arc from the guard position to your own center line, twisting your torso to the right. Quickly reverse the action, thrusting your right hip forward, then the right shoulder and right arm in an arc to your own center line, pulling the left arm back into the guard position.

Forward Lateral Strike — This is done much as a hook punch, and may be done with the reverse, lead, or lunge method, and with the drop step technique. Elbow strikes are generally done to the head or solar plexus for instant results; the forward lateral strike is a high level attack. In a left Fighting stance with the hands in a mid level guard, pull the right fist up tight to the right bicep, snap the right hip forward sharply and straighten the right leg. Throw the right shoulder forward, twisting the torso to the left, and bring the right elbow up to your own center line, high level in an arc. Now repeat the sequence with the left elbow for a lead strike, but use the drop step method by lifting the heel of the left foot as you snap the hip to the right. Stamp the heel down as you strike with the elbow.

Across the Body Strike — In a left Straddle stance, with the hands in the mid level guard, pull the left fist to the right shoulder, cocking the hips to the right, and turning the torso slightly to the right. Snap the hips to the left, then the torso and left shoulder, then the arm. Keep the left forearm tightly against the left upper arm and strike with the upper striking area of the elbow to the high level on your own center line. The upper striking arm is from the tip to approximately four inches above it. At the end of this strike the left fist is in front of, and even with, the left shoulder. This may be done from any of the stances in a lead or lunge method, generally after blocking, and

Across the body elbow strike

Rising elbow strike

Downward elbow strike

Rear elbow strike

may be done with the drop step technique also.

Rising Strike — From a right Fighting stance with the hands in the mid level guard, pull the right hip back, as though throwing an uppercut or scooping with a shovel. Cock the torso slightly to the right also, and hold the right forearm tightly against the right bicep. Thrust the right hip forward with the scooping motion, twist the torso forward and straighten the left leg, then arc the elbow forward and upward to your own center line, striking with the lower surface of the striking point. This is from the tip approximately four inches downward. This may be done in the lead, reverse, or lunge method from any stance, as well as to the flanks.

Downward Strike — From a left Fighting stance with the hands in the mid level guard, raise the left arm slightly, holding the left forearm tightly against the left bicep. Cock the hips to the left and raise the left foot slightly. Drive the hip forward and downward, then the shoulder, and the elbow. As you strike downward, stomp the left foot downward, too. Use the lower striking point. This may be done from most of the stances in the lead, reverse, and lunge methods as well as to the flanks.

Rear Strike — This strike pistons straight backward. From a right Fighting stance with the hands in the mid level guard, extend the left hand straight forward, turning the hips to the right. Strike straight backward with the arm, bending it as it nears the target point and holding the left forearm tightly against the left bicep. Strike with the upper striking point. Snap the hips to the left as you strike. This may be done from any stance with either the lead or reverse arm. Often, to get the proper range, you will have to step backward into the opponent, which adds momentum to your strike.

Training Routines

You may do these as "shadow fighting", but it is more advantageous to strike a heavy punching bag with these techniques to get the feel of them when you strike with power, and to condition your elbow for impact. Each routine should be done ten times at least, trying at all times to use proper tension, body rotation, and focus. Tense at the completion of each strike. Add speed when you are able to perform the technique correctly. Then begin to work out your own combination of elbow strikes, using them in other training phases detailed later.

(1) Stand in a left Fighting stance with the hands in a mid level guard. Hook across the body with a right lateral elbow strike. As you draw it back into the guard, strike with a left lateral strike. Change to a right Fighting stance and repeat the strikes.

From fighting stance into reverse lateral elbow strike

(2) Stand in a right Fighting stance with the hands in a mid level guard. Strike with a left rising strike followed rapidly with a right lateral strike. Follow this with a rapid left lateral strike, then a right rising strike. Change stances to a left Fighting stance and repeat the routine.

(3) Form a left Straddle stance, hands in the mid level guard. Strike with a left across the body strike, then pull the hands back to the guard and perform a left downward strike. Pivot on the ball of the left foot clockwise, stepping the right foot to your left forward so that you are positioned with your back to the heavy bag or the opponent, forming a front Straddle stance. Strike the bag with a right rear strike. Pivot on the ball of the right foot in a clockwise direction so that the right side is now facing the bag, stepping the left foot around and forming a right Straddle stance, hands in the mid level guard. Perform a right across the body strike, pull the arm back, and perform a right downward strike. Pivot on the ball of the right foot stepping the left foot to your right rear forming a front Straddle stance, your back to the opponent or the heavy bag. Strike with a left rear strike.

The Knees

The knee, like the elbow, is often overlooked as a source of offense and defense in martial arts because it does not have the range a kick or hand technique has. But like the elbow, it can generate great power to a small impact area and it serves to power many other techniques. Its defensive use is covered in the blocking section. In offense it is supremely valuable during in-fighting. It is susceptible to injuries like the elbow, and is more often a target for the opponent because of its value in supporting a fighter. If one knee is damaged you cannot kick or even move very effectively in a fight. Be aware of this and guard your knees.

Knee kicks are done with a springing motion of the foot beginning the strike. Lift the heel so that the foot rests on the ball, then suddenly spring upward or laterally into one of the knee kicks. To practice knee kicks, mix them in with your hand and elbow training techniques after you understand the basic principles of the spring attack. Exercises to strengthen the legs and hips for kicking also strengthen the legs for knee kicks.

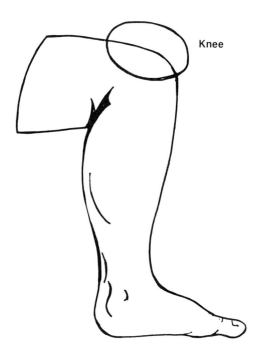

Knee

Rising Knee Kick — From a left Fighting stance with the hands in the close range guard, raise the heel of the right foot and cock the hips to the right. Thrust the right hip forward, spring off the ball of the right foot and drive the right knee upward and forward to your own center line. When striking the groin or bent head of the opponent, the higher you drive the knee, the harder the blow will land. This may be done from most stances with either the lead or reverse legs. It is often most effective to strike the opponent in the mid level. Reach out and grasp his head, and thrust it downward into the rising knee kick. The bladder and belly are also targets of this technique. The striking point is just above the knee cap itself.

Round Knee Kick — From a right Fighting stance with the hands in the close range guard, raise the heel of the left foot and cock the hips to the left. This knee kick moves in an arc just like a hook punch or a round kick. Snap the hips to the right, spring the foot upward off the ball, and attack in an arc with the knee to your own center line. The lower leg is pulled tightly to the side of the thigh and not below it as in the rising knee kick, the striking point being the same.

Kicking Techniques

Any practical fighting art must by definition include some type of kicking technique. Most styles of karate originally used low kicks, rarely ever above the waist, but when they became ways as opposed to methods they began to develop higher kicks. Kicking techniques have their greatest range at your own waist level; lower or higher and they begin to lose range. However, this is not to say that they are not effective. You may train to use head kicks as well as shin or knee kicks; both have their use in fighting. To begin training, however, try to use waist high kicks.

Effective kicking methods are more difficult to learn than other striking methods, for the kicks employ the body in such a manner that they use the greatest possible force from positions having the least available base of support. They call for the agility of a dancer in combination with such speed and concentration of force that they are unparalleled in any other sport or exercise. The back and stomach muscles must be strenthened to help generate the force which is transmitted into the striking foot. All kicking motion, like most other techniques, starts with the hip. The kicking foot may be thought of as the tip of a long, subtle ship, having in itself little weight or strength but which transmits all of the energy, augmented many times by the acceleration of progressively contracting muscles of the wielder into tremendous force. For this reason the hip requires special attention.

Round knee kick

Rising knee kick

Good hip flexibility first of all requires familiarity with the range of movement in the hip joint. Hip flexibility will give you smoother and stronger mobility as well as stationary hip-weight shifting (moving from one stance to another without stepping, for example) and ease of movement when shifting directions. Listed next are some special exercises taken from dance for the hip. They may be difficult to do at first, but done regularly and for several weeks they will loosen and strengthen the hips to give you all of the benefits of movement and kicking ability that you desire.

(1) Begin by lying on your back, hands flat on the floor beside you. Raise your right leg bending the knee until the right foot is at the level of the left knee. Keep your left leg straight and flat on the floor and your head flat on the floor. Slowly, rotate your right leg outward as far as it will go, then bring it back to the upright position. The knee has described an arc. Repeat this ten times, then straighten the leg and raise the left one, performing the same exercise.

(2) Lay flat on your back with your arms spread out slightly from your sides, but flat on the floor, and your legs comfortably spread as far as you can. With both legs straight at the knee, raise the right leg a foot off the floor and make a side-to-side figure eight with the foot. Make ten large eights, and then ten smaller ones, about half the width of the bigger ones, then reverse the direction and repeat the entire sequence. Lower the right leg and do the same with the left leg, then repeat with the right until you have performed the exercise ten times on each leg.

(3) Begin in the same spread eagle position as number two. Bend both knees until the toes of each foot meet in the middle, knees bent outward. Push both knees sideways to the floor and try to lift both hips off the ground. Strain at this movement for a moment, then relax. Repeat this twenty times. Most people will not be able to get their knees to the ground when they first begin, so do not be discouraged if you cannot. Perseverance will pay off, though.

Balance

Adequate balance must be maintained to withstand the shock of impact when your kick meets its target, as you will be standing on only one leg. The supporting foot, which bears the entire weight of your body, must be securely placed so that you are not pushed over backward, or your foot pulled out from under you. Balance must be held so that it does not nullify your momentum, but adds to it. For example, if you are leaning backward when you kick to the front your movement will lose strength and you may fall over backward from the impact. Leaning too far forward causes you to fall forward into your target. You should be standing upright and leaning slightly forward, not away from the target, when you kick.

Practice multiple kicks while standing on one leg. When you begin this, lean against a chair or tree for support, but as your skill increases do not lean on anything. You may perform the kicks in any sequence that you desire; several front kicks, a front kick, then a round kick, then a side kick. It is up to you.

Hand positioning also aids in balance when kicking. Keep your guard up when you kick, extending the hand forward on the side that is kicking to aid balance. If you find a more comfortable position to hold the hands, as long as it is practical, use it. Generally, the mid level or close range guards are the best way to hold your hands when you kick.

Warm Up — The legs need to be exercised lightly before they are put to any strenuous use because of the strain put on them in kicking. If they are not warmed up at all, you may pull a muscle. Warming up simply means to pump blood into the muscles gradually, loosening them up for more activity. Useful warmups are listed in the calisthenics section.

Reach — Perhaps the most obvious advantage of the kicking technique is that the legs are longer and stronger than the arms and thus give the fighter greater reach. Not all kicks have the same reach, of course; some are for closer range than others, just as hand techniques are designed for different ranges. Lengthening a kick is mostly a matter of body mechanics. Rear leg kicks are generally stronger and longer than front leg kicks, and any kick obtains its maximum range at your own waist height. Keep this in mind when training.

Recovery — After you execute a kick you must return the kicking leg to the chambered position and then to the floor quickly. This prevents your leg from being grabbed while it is in the air, and allows you to continue to attack quickly. Withdraw the leg to the chamber with *greater* force than you kicked with, then step back or forward, but do not just drop your leg into position and fall forward or backward.

During both kicking and recovery, keep the knee of the supporting leg slightly bent. This provides greater support for the upper body and lessens the chance of damage to the supporting knee if it is attacked while the other leg is in the air.

Three Types of Kicks — There are three types of kicks: snap, thrust, and sweep. Snap kicks are fast kicks that penetrate but do not produce tremendous shock force, leaving the opponent standing in front of you, usually doubled over. Thrust kicks are a little slower,

Ball

Instep

Sword edge

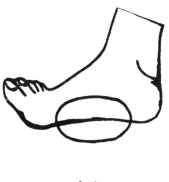

Arch

but knock the opponent away or stop his movement cold. Sweep kicks hit with a forceful slap and turn the opponent. They have the capability to inflict serious damage to the opponent, as do all kicking techniques.

The Kicks

There are two kinds of front kicks, the front snap and the front thrust, with three methods of delivery for each.

(1) Front Snap Kick — Form a Ready stance with the hands in the mid level guard. Raise the right leg, bent at the knee with the lower leg tucked tightly against the rear of the thigh. Raise the knee as high as you can. Even in a low kick, the higher you can raise the knee the more force will be applied to the target. As you raise the knee, cock the right hip to the right. Snap the hip forward, then the leg, letting the lower leg uncoil from the upper leg like a whip. When the right leg is extended, snap the right hip *back,* causing the whip-like cracking effect in the kick. After the hip is retracted, bring the lower leg back to the coiled, chambered position, tucked beneath the upper leg. The striking point is either the ball of the foot with the foot extended forward, toes curled back, or the instep of the foot, with the toes lowered. Use the instep only when attacking the groin area. Just before impact tighten (tense) the ankle.

Rear Leg Kick — Form a right Fighting stance with the hands in the mid level guard and perform a front snap kick with the left leg, lifting the foot from the floor heel first, then springing off the floor with the ball into the chambered position for the kick. Snap it out, rechamber it, then set it down with the left foot forward forming a left Fighting stance. Perform a rear leg right front snap kick. This kick has the greatest power and range of the three front kick methods. Keep the supporting leg bent during the kick. The knee aims this kick. When you raise the thigh to kick and chamber the lower leg, wherever the knee is pointed is where the kick is going. When you shift your weight onto the lead leg to kick, the movement may alert your opponent so that weight shift-chamber-kick actions must be performed smoothly and rapidly, seeming to blend together.

Front Leg Kick — From a right Fighting stance with the hands in the mid level guard, shift your weight onto your rear leg. Cock your hips to the right and raise the right foot, heel first, then spring upward into the chambered position. Snap the lower leg outward, then rechamber it using proper hip rotation during the kick. This kick is faster than the rear leg kick, but may not have as much power. It is often used for a low level jab to distract the opponent, to check his kick attack, or to close the gap. It can be very powerful, however,

Front Snap Kick
(1) From fighting stance

(2) Chamber kicking leg by bringing rear leg forward

(3) Snap kick out

(4) Rechamber leg

particularly if you catch the opponent coming in toward you.

Foot Replacement Kick — Assume a right Fighting stance with the hands in the mid level guard. Using the foot replacement method of stepping, bring the left foot to the right, then chamber the right foot and deliver a right front snap kick. The foot replacement technique adds momentum and power to the front kick and it is very deceptive for attacks. It may also be used in retreat.

Assume a left Fighting stance with the hands in the mid level guard. Bring the left foot back to the right using the foot replacement method and chamber the right foot. Deliver a right front snap kick. Use the same principles as for a rear leg front snap kick.

(2) Front Thrust Kick — Form a Ready stance with the hands in the mid level guard. Raise the right leg and chamber it in the same way that the snap kick is chambered, cocking the hips to the right. Thrust the right hip forward followed by the right leg. Thrust, don't snap, the lower leg forward from the chamber. Do not retract the hip as you did in the snap kick, allow the thrusting foot to drive into the target. Retract the leg as strongly as you thrust it out, then place the foot down to form a Ready stance. Repeat the kick with the left leg.

The front thrust kick may be done with the lead or reverse leg, or in the foot replacement method with the same attributes as the front snap kick, the striking point being either the ball of the foot or the instep.

There are two kinds of side kicks, the side snap, and the side thrust.

(1) Side Snap Kick — Assume a Ready stance with the hands in a right mid level guard (as though you were in a right Straddle stance with the head turned to the right). Lift the heel of the right foot, then the ball, lifting the thigh and bending the knee. Pull the foot inward toward the left knee, but not touching it, and point the bent knee and thigh to the right. Cock the hips slightly to the left. Snap the hips, then the leg to the right, allowing the lower leg to uncoil from the chambered position to the right and full extension. As the leg reaches full extension, retract the right hip, creating the whip-like effect. The striking area is the blade edge of the right foot, from the base of the little toe to the heel, so the foot must be turned sideways and the toes raised to give the foot and ankle the proper attitude. Retract the lower leg to the chambered position, then place it beside the left foot forming a Ready stance. Perform a left side snap kick with the left leg.

Rear Leg Kick — Form a right Fighting stance with the hands in the mid level guard. Shift your weight onto your right leg, raise the heel of the left foot, spring off the floor from the ball of the foot and into the chambered position. As you pull the left lower leg into

Side Kick
(1) Start in fighting stance

(2) Advance rear leg, chamber kick

(3) Kick, then rechamber leg

chamber, pivot clockwise on the ball of your right foot so that the raised left knee points straight forward. Snap the hips and leg forward (to the left) into a left snap kick, rechamber the leg and place it down forward forming a left Fighting stance. Perform a right rear leg side snap kick. Some people have the tendency to raise their arms over their head during a side kick. Refrain from doing this. Keep both hands in the mid level guard. You may extend the hand on the kicking side, but do not raise it into the air. The rear leg kick may be done from any stance.

Front Leg Kick — Form a left Fighting stance with the hands in the mid level guard. Raise the heel of the left foot and chamber the left lower leg for a side snap kick. Pivot to your right on the ball of your right foot until the knee of the chambered left leg is pointing straight ahead, and attack with a left side snap kick. Rechamber the leg and put it down to your left rear forming a right Fighting stance, then perform a right front leg side snap kick. This may be done from any stance.

Foot Replacement Kick — Form a right Fighting stance with the hands in the mid level guard. Bring the left foot to the right in the foot replacement method, turning the left foot, toes to the left at a ninety degree angle to the right foot. Quickly chamber the right leg and perform a right snap kick straight forward. This is a very quick movement and the foot replacement may be done as a skip or jump motion. The basic motions of the side snap kick should be understood thoroughly before the foot replacement kick should be learned. It offers greater range and power than any other kick.

(2) Side Thrust Kick — Assume a Ready stance with the hands in the mid level guard. Lift the heel of the right foot, then spring upward off the ball, chambering your right leg in exactly the same way you would for a right side snap kick. Snap the hips to the right, then extend the right leg, uncoiling the lower leg. Do not retract the hip when the leg is at full extension; drive the foot into the target. After you tense at the moment of focus, withdraw the lower leg and rechamber it, then place the right foot beside the left foot, forming a Ready stance. Perform a left side thrust kick. The striking area is the same as in the side snap kick.

The side thrust kick may be done with the lead or reverse legs in the same manner that the side snap kick is performed, and it may be done with a foot replacement just like the side snap kick. The thrust kick is very effective for knee kicks and for checking kicks to the opponent's legs or body. It has a greater striking area surface (blade edge of the foot) than the front kick (ball of the foot), and is less likely to slip off a bent knee than is a front kick, either kicking into the front or side of it to damage the knee, or stomping the back of the knee to effect a take down.

There are two rear kicks, the snap and the thrust.

(1) Rear Snap Kick — From a Ready stance, look over your left shoulder to the straight rear. Raise the heel of the left foot, then snap the rear of the heel up and back in an arc. Do not move the thigh very much to the rear, the kick comes up but not back very far. The striking area is the rear of the heel, the kick generally being applied to the groin of the opponent, though it may also be used to strike into his shin. It is a quick technique that gathers its strength from the speed of delivery and not its wind up or hip movement.

The rear snap kick may be performed from the lead or the reverse leg, with the thigh swinging the lower leg backward and upward if the lead leg is used. It is not particularly complicated and is best used at close range, when the opponent has grappled with you. It may be used with the foot replacement method also, bringing the lead leg to the rear leg, then kicking with the rear leg for added momentum, but again, this must be done quickly to be effective.

(2) Rear Thrust Kick — Begin in a Ready stance with the hands in the mid level guard. Look over your left shoulder to the straight rear and lift the heel of the left foot. Lift the left foot and chamber it as though for a front kick, and cock the foot as though for a left side kick. The striking area is both the bottom rear of the heel and the rear blade edge of the foot. Snap your hips to the left rear and drive the left leg straight backward, twisting the torso to the left rear. This kick is performed as a thrust kick with no retraction of the hip at focus. After the moment of tension, rechamber the leg and place it beside the right foot forming a Ready stance. Perform a rear thrust kick with the right leg. This kick is particularly effective to the bladder area, and the solar plexus as the opponent is coming at you from behind, but has not yet closed the gap. It may be used against the face also.

It may be performed with either the rear or the lead leg in much the same manner that the rear snap kick is performed, and in the foot replacement method also.

Spin Rear Thrust Kick — Form a right Fighting stance with the hands in the mid level guard. Use the Glide step method to step the left foot diagonally to your right front. Chamber the right leg for a rear thrust kick and pivot simultaneously on the ball of the left foot. Spin as fast as you can 180 degrees clockwise so that your back is to what began as your straight forward, and attack with a right rear thrust kick.

Spin Rear Thrust Kick
(1) Start in fighting stance

(2) Spin 360 degrees clockwise, chambering rear leg for kick

(3) Kick, then rechamber leg

To retreat using this kick, form a right Fighting stance with the hands in the mid level guard. Use the cross stepping method and step your right foot in front of your left foot to your left rear. Rotate your torso and chamber your left leg for a rear thrust kick, pivoting on the ball of your right foot 180 degrees counterclockwise, attacking with a left rear thrust kick.

After both kicks, rechamber the leg. Do not let it fall to the ground anywhere. Do not let the force of your spin pull you too far off balance. When you kick, you must have control of your body. If you miss, you will fall into the kick if you let it pull you along with it. This is a very powerful kick, especially if you catch your opponent stepping in with it. It is also very deceptive. If your opponent has never seen a spinning technique before, when you spin it will baffle him. An excellent follow up for this kick is a backfist as you kick. Strike with the same side arm that the kicking leg is on.

Round Kick — This kick travels from the side of the body into the opponent's side in a semi-circular arc with a whipping snap. Form a Ready stance with the hands in the mid level guard. Raise the right foot, heel first, then the ball, then the lower leg. Bring it to the outside of the right thigh so that the right foot is tucked against the side of the right buttock. Cock the hips to the right. Snap the hips forward and to the left, simultaneously pivoting on the ball of the left foot so the toes of the left foot face the left (counterclockwise), then whip the right thigh forward and then the lower leg. Just before the lower leg reaches full extension, retract the right hip creating the whipping effect of a snap kick. Turn the torso to the left with the kick. Retract the leg to the chamber and place it on the floor forming a Ready stance. Perform a left leg round kick. The striking area is either the ball of the foot with the toes curled back or the area between the instep and the lower shin. This area is used for kicking the outside of the opponent's thigh or the side of his knee, not the torso. At completion of the kick, the foot is turned so that the outside of the kicking foot ankle is turned up, the toes turned to the side. (For example, the right round kick would have the toes turned to the left.)

Rear Leg Kick — From a right Fighting stance, chamber the left leg for a left round kick. Snap the kick forward, pivoting on the ball of the right foot, kicking to your own center line. Retract the kick and form a left Fighting stance, then perform a right rear leg round kick.

Front Leg Kick — From a right Fighting stance, shift your weight onto your left leg and chamber the right leg for a right round kick. Cock your hips to the right as you chamber the kick. Snap the kick forward to your own center line, twisting your torso to the left with the kick and pivoting on the ball of the left foot. The lead leg kick is not as strong as the rear leg kick, but it may be faster, used much as a leading side hook punch is used, to sneak in behind the opponent's guard.

Foot Replacement Kick — Assume a left Fighting stance with the hands in the mid level guard. Bring the right foot to the left foot in the foot replacement method and quickly chamber the left foot for a lead leg round kick. Snap the kick out, pivoting on the ball of the right foot and twisting the torso to the right with the kick. Retract the kick and form a Ready stance.

Outside Crescent Kick — This kick moves from the floor to the target in a high arcing trajectory which describes a crescent. Form a Ready stance with the hands in the mid level guard, then extend the left hand with the palm facing to the right, fingers open. Raise the heel of the right foot, and snap the hips to the left as you bring the foot upward from the floor to your own center line in an arc, striking the palm of your left hand with the arch of your right foot. Leave the knee of the right leg bent slightly and tense the ankle of the right foot at impact. Retract the right leg by bending the right knee and chambering the right leg as though for a front kick, then replace it beside the left foot forming a Ready stance. Extend the right hand, raise the heel of the left foot, snap the hips to the right, and perform a left outside crescent kick.

This kick is useful as a strike at close range where the opponent would not normally be expecting a kick, and it is deceptive. It may also be used for a block.

Rear Leg Kick — Form a right Fighting stance with the hands in the mid level guard. Shift your weight to your right leg as you raise the left foot onto the ball. Snap your hips to the right and bring the left leg in an arc to your own center line, tensing your left ankle at impact. Bend the knee of the left leg, stepping forward into a left Fighting stance. Perform a right rear leg crescent kick.

Front Leg Kick — Form a left Fighting stance with the hands in the mid level guard. Shift your weight onto your right rear leg as you raise the heel of the left foot. Snap your hips to the right as you bring your left leg upward to your own center line. Retract the kick and form a right Fighting stance, then perform a right leg outside crescent kick. This kick has more range than a rear leg kick, and is faster to perform since it has less distance to travel to the opponent than a rear leg kick does.

Foot Replacement Kick — Form a left Fighting stance with the hands in the mid level guard. Using the foot replacement method, bring the right foot to the left, then raise the left foot onto the ball, and snap the hips to the right. Bring your foot upward in an arc to your own center line, and retract it, forming a right Fighting stance. Using the foot replacement method, perform a right outside crescent kick. The foot replacement method is often used for closing the gap with this kick since it is essentially a close range attack.

Inside Crescent Kick — The inside crescent kick is for very close range. Its power comes from the downward momentum of its arc. Form a Ready stance with the hands in the mid level guard, then extend the left hand with the palm facing to the right, fingers open. Raise the heel of the left foot and snap the hips to the left, then bring the left foot to the right. As you snap your hips to the left, snap the left foot, cocked as though for a side kick, in an arc from its position near the floor in a high arc, then downward into the palm of your open left hand.

Keep the knee of the left leg bent at impact. To rechamber the kick, bend the knee of the left leg and chamber it as though for a front kick. Set it down beside the right foot forming a Ready stance, then perform a right inside crescent kick.

Rear Leg Kick — Form a left Fighting stance with the hands in the mid level guard. Raise the heel of the right foot and swing the foot to the left, in front of the left foot. Snap the hips to the right, and arc the right foot up and to the right, coming downward with a sharp snap into the palm of your extended right hand or into a heavy bag. Rechamber the leg and step forward into a right Fighting stance, then perform a left leg inside crescent kick.

Front Leg Kick — Form a right Fighting stance with the hands in the mid level guard. Shift your weight onto your left leg, raise the heel of the right foot, and swing it to the left. Snap your hips to the right and snap your leg upward and inward in an arc. Rechamber the leg and step into a left Fighting stance, performing a left leg inside crescent kick.

Foot Replacement Kick — Form a left Fighting stance with the hands in the mid level guard. Using the foot replacement method, bring the right foot to the left foot, then raise the heel of the left foot, and swing it to the right. Snap your hips to the left and perform a left inside crescent kick. This is often used to close the gap in attack as this is an extremely close range technique.

Training Methods

Begin by learning each kick separately on a heavy punching bag. Kick the bag with full power, trying to drive the foot through the bag with focus, proper tension and power. Get the feel of snapping the hips into each technique. Perform each kick on each leg so that you develop both sides of your body equally. When you begin training perform ten of each kick on each leg, gradually adding a few repetitions until you are able to perform fifty repetitions without pause. Your endurance for a real fight will be increased dramatically.

After you have a firm understanding of each individual technique, begin putting them together in combinations. Three kicks to one combination are generally as many as are safe, without the opponent being able to predict what is coming next. Some examples are as follow:

(1) From a left Fighting stance with the hands in the mid level guard, perform a low level front snap kick, rechamber the kick and set the foot forward. As soon as it touches the floor, attack with a low level rear leg right side kick. Rechamber the right leg and set it forward in a right Front stance. Reach forward with your hands as though grasping and pulling something to you, and attack with a left knee kick.

(2) From a right Fighting stance, attack with a right side kick. Rechamber the leg and place it forward; as soon as it touches the floor, attack with a mid or low level left round kick. Rechamber the leg and place it forward, then attack with a right mid level front kick.

(3) From a left Fighting stance with the hands in the mid level guard, attack with a left inside crescent kick, then rechamber the leg, setting it down in the same stance. Attack with a right outside crescent kick, and rechamber the leg. Set the foot down to form a right Straddle stance and attack with a right side kick.

Effective kicking may also include using the same foot to attack without replacing it on the floor. Two kicks in this manner are sufficient.

(1) From a left leading Fighting stance with the hands in the mid level guard, attack with a front kick to the low level. Rechamber the leg without putting the foot on the floor, then pivot on the supporting leg and attack with a side kick.

(2) From a right Fighting stance with the hands in the mid level guard, attack with a right outside crescent kick. Rechamber the leg without touching the floor with the foot, pivot on the ball of the left foot, and attack with a right side kick.

(3) From a left Fighting stance with the hands in the mid level guard, attack with a low level left round kick. Rechamber the leg and attack the mid level with a left round kick.

(4) From a right Fighting stance with the hands in the mid level

guard, attack with a right front snap kick to the low level, rechamber the leg, and attack with a right round kick to the mid level.

Fighting Combinations

Kicks are stronger but slower than hand techniques. To be totally effective in defense situations they are set up by either a block-evasion, or a hand strike. A person that has trained only in kicks may be defeated if the opponent is able to jam or evade his first kick; equally a person that has trained only in the use of hand techniques may be defeated with a well placed kick. To be combat efficient, one must learn to integrate the two in combinations. One sets the other up; a kick may help you to close the gap with the opponent for a hand technique or vice versa. In training it should be stressed that the two are inseparable. Some examples of these combinations are listed below:

(1) From a left Fighting stance, with the hands in the mid level guard, attack with a left leading straight punch. As soon as the punch retracts from the high level, attack with a right rear leg front snap kick to the low level. Retract the kick and step forward into a right Front stance and attack the high level with a right forward lateral elbow strike.

(2) From a right Fighting stance with the hands in the mid level guard, attack with a left backfist strike to the high level. As the fist returns to the guard, attack with a left side kick to the low level. Rechamber the leg and step forward to form a left Front stance and strike with a right middle single knuckle fist to the mid level.

(3) From a right Fighting stance with the hands in the mid level guard, attack with a high level left straight punch. As the hand returns to the guard position, attack the low level with a right round kick. As the foot touches the floor attack the high level with a right across the body backfist.

(4) From a left Fighting stance attack the high level with a flat spear hand. As the hand returns to the guard, attack with a right outside crescent kick. Rechamber the kick and place the foot to the left forward. Pivot on the ball of the right foot and execute a spin rear thrust kick to the low level. Attack with an across the body backfist with the left hand as you complete the kick.

These are just a few of the hundreds of possible combinations that may be used in actual combat. Learn each technique separately and begin to combine them in training. When they begin to come together naturally for you, work on accuracy in striking, and power. Do not sacrifice power for speed.

"Defense and Offense Are One"
Blocking Technique

Effective blocking is essential for self-defense. You must be able to stop your opponent from hitting you without having to move out of your own effective hitting range. If you are not able to stop your opponent from hitting you, it is doubtful that you will be able to counterattack at all. In real combat your opponent may be faster, stronger, or more aggressive than you and it is hard to stop all of the strikes of such opponents. Without training in the proper methods of blocking and repetitive drills in the applications of blocking it may be impossible.

Most blocking techniques use the same body mechanics that strikes do, so that the blocks will damage the opponent. The energy of the defender is concentrated to meet the force of the attacker with the shock force of a strike either injuring the offending limb as it enters your defensive perimeter or moving the opponent so that he overextends himself, allowing the forward momentum he has created to pull him off balance. This may negate the need for counterattacks, but if it does not you are in an ideal position for follow-up technique. To avoid off-balancing yourself while blocking, all blocks end in a position parallel with the outer extremes of your body. Never over-extend a block.

Hard Blocks

Rising Forearm Block — Form a right Fighting stance with the hands in the mid level guard. Your training partner stands in front of you then steps forward with his right foot and attacks your head with a right overhead Hammer fist blow. As he attacks, slide your left foot forward and form a left Front stance. Lower the left arm across your body to the right to the level of your right hip, cocking your hips to the right. When you step and cock the hips it should all be one fluid motion. Snap your hips to the left with a thrusting motion of your lower abdomen and snap your left arm upward, rotating the forearm and hand so that the bony lower edge (little finger edge) of your forearm strikes the opponent's arm either at the wrist, which may cause his hand to open involuntarily if he is armed with a weapon; or just above his elbow which will snap his arm straight, injuring his arm.

At the completion of the block your forearm should be slightly higher than your forehead and at approximately a sixty degree angle to your upper arm, from the premise that your forearm is at a ninety degree

Rising Block with Reverse Punch
(1) Aggressor stalks victim.

(2) Aggressor pulls knife, defender assumes fighting stance

(3) Defender uses left rising block against attacker's lunge with knife

(4) (a.) Rising block with reverse vertical fist punch to attacker's 'base of sternum.' (Number 20 on Vital Striking Areas, Chapter 4)

4 (b.) She is in front fighting stance, left hand performing outer deflection block, right spear hand to eye of attacker

4 (c.) Her left hand perfoming outer deflection block, front kick to attackers bladder, her right hand remains chambered in mid level guard.

Outer Forearm Block

Completed Rising Block

angle to your upper arm when held out straight and at a forty-five degree angle when bent straight across your forehead. This is important because if your arm is at a forty-five degree angle across your forehead when you strike his arm, your forearm will absorb the full impact of his blow. At a sixty degree angle, his blow will slide off of your arm obliquely. As with a strike, at the moment of impact, bring the entire body to tension and exhale. The blocking hand may be open or clenched into a fist, and it may be performed with either the lead hand or the reverse hand as the situation demands. It may also be used against a straight strike, not just an overhead attack.

Outer Forearm Block — Form a left Fighting stance with your hands in the mid level guard. Your opponent attacks with a left straight punch to your face. Step your right foot to your right front forming an angular Straddle stance. As you step, pull your left forearm to your right shoulder, cocking your hips to the right. Snap your hips to the left and strike with your left forearm to your left, into his forearm. Turn into a right Back stance as you block. Rotate the forearm so that the thin bony outer edge (little finger edge) strikes his arm. The blocking hand should be closed into a fist. At the moment of impact tense the body and exhale. Blocking in this manner, sidestepping the attack and then striking into it, puts you outside his strike and he is unable to strike you again without stepping. You on the other hand, have off-balanced him and are in good position to strike him.

The second method of using this block is straight ahead. Your opponent strikes with a right straight punch to your face level. Pull your left forearm to your right shoulder and cock your hips to the right. Snap your hips to the left and strike into his forearm with the lower edge of your forearm. This method opens the opponent's center line for a counterattack.

Low Level Sweep Block — In a right Fighting stance with the hands in the mid level guard, the opponent attacks with a right front kick to your groin area. Cross your right forearm over your left arm, right hand going to your left shoulder and slide the right foot forward forming a right Front stance. As you cross your arm to the left cock your hips to the left also. Snap your hips to the right and strike downward with a sweeping motion of your right arm into the opponent's lower leg, fist closed. Do not let your arm go beyond the right knee. When you strike the opponent's leg, tense the entire body and exhale. The thin bony outer edge of your forearm is the impact surface (little finger edge).

By blocking with the same side arm as he is kicking with (block his right leg with your right arm), you will turn him away from you,

Sequence For Low Level Sweep Block
(1)

(2)

(3)

opening his side up to any strike you desire to deliver. Blocking with the opposite side arm will open his center line.

This same block may be done with the sword edge of the hand, striking into the opponent's leg with the hand itself instead of the forearm. The motion of the block is the same.

Deflection Blocks

Deflecting an opponent's strike is often faster and more useful than hard blocks. A deflection redirects the force of the blow without meeting that same force head on and is considered a "soft" block. They are performed with the same body mechanics as all other techniques, hip first, and tension at impact.

Outer Deflection Block — Stand in a left Fighting stance with the hands in the mid level guard. The opponent stands in front of you and attacks with a right face level punch. Pull your left hand back to your right shoulder, cocking your hips to the right, palm of the hand facing your chest and the hand open. Snap your hips to the left and bring your left forearm to the left, rotating the hand so that the sword edge strikes the opponent's wrist or forearm, with your palm facing him at the completion of the block. Do not let your hand go beyond your left shoulder. This block is done close to the body.

This block may be used to stop across the body strikes also. If the opponent attacks with a left backfist, strike across his body. The block is performed the same way, with your left hand striking into his forearm with the sword edge. This torques the right, reverse side into a counterstrike.

There are three uses for the **Inner Deflection Blocks:** across the body high level, across the body mid level, and the beat.

(1) Across the Body (high level) — In a left Fighting stance with the hands in the mid level guard, the opponent attacks with a left face level punch. Snap your hips to the left and strike into the opponent's arm with the right palm, in the same manner that a palm fist thrust is used. It is very similar to a close range hook punch. Do not go beyond the left shoulder with the block. This chambers the left side for a counterblow, turning the hips for a wind up to the left side blow, or for an across the body strike with the right hand.

(2) Across the Body (mid level) — Form a right Fighting stance with the hands in the mid level guard. The opponent attacks with a right straight punch to your solar plexus area. Snap your hips to the right and strike into his forearm with your left palm fist, thrusting his right arm down and to your right so that it passes below your right elbow. Do not thrust past the right side of your body. This winds your body

Outer Deflection Block

Sequence for Inner Deflection High Level Block
(1)

(2) Inner deflection begins

(3) Deflection completed

up for an across the body counter with the left hand or a right hand attack.

(3) The Beat — Form a left Fighting stance with the hands in the mid level guard. The opponent attacks with a right straight punch to your face level. Strike into his forearm with your left palm fist, forcing his arm downward and to your right, but remove your hand from his arm as soon as the force of his strike is redirected. Return it to the guard position or counterattack with it immediately. The hand rebounds from his arm. An across the body backfist would be appropriate.

Low Level Block — Form a left Fighting stance with the hands in the mid level guard. The opponent attacks your groin area with a right front kick. Snap the hips to the left and snap the left forearm downward, striking the opponent's leg with the left palm fist, palm turned to face your left. This slaps the opponent's leg out of the way, off-balancing him and opening his center line to counterattack. Quickly, return the hand to the guard position, or counterattack with the right side quickly.

Elbow Blocks

The elbows are efficient for blocking and are often overlooked in fighting systems. When your hands are in the mid level guard position they are in a natural position for close lateral blocking which requires very little movement.

Forward Elbow Block — In a right Fighting stance with the hands in the mid level guard your opponent attacks with a right punch to your head. Twist forward and to the right with your hips and strike into his forearm with your left elbow, bringing it up and forward in a circular motion. Your left hand rotates in toward your chin. The contact point is the area just below your elbow.

Side Elbow Block — In a left Fighting stance with the hands in the mid level guard the opponent attacks with a left hook punch to the ribs. Drive your right elbow down and backward so that it strikes the opponent's forearm between his wrist and elbow. This is particularly effective against a round kick to your rib area, but is equally effective against hook punches.

Knee and Kick Blocks

Knee Sweep — Your opponent attacks with a front snap kick to your groin area with his right leg. Quickly raise your right knee upward until the thigh is parallel to the floor and sweep it into his right knee or thigh, redirecting his kick from your center line to your left.

Inner Deflection Mid Level Block

Low level palm fist block

A variation of this is to strike into his thigh with your right knee at an angle (left forward) as he raises his knee to kick you. Perform a knee kick into his thigh to left forward with your right knee, then attack his supporting leg with a low level side snap kick.

Knee Jam — As the opponent chambers for any kind of kick, lunge forward and strike into his upper thigh or hip area with a knee kick which not only jams his kick, but knocks him off balance.

Kick Block — As your opponent chambers for a front kick, pivot toward him and attack the shin or ankle of his kicking leg with a side thrust kick. This is usually done with a rear leg pivoting side kick.

Grabbing Blocks

You should practice grabbing the opponent after every block to control or off-balance him. There are two blocks that are designed for control at contact.

Scoop Block — In a left Fighting stance with your hands in a mid level guard your opponent attacks with a right straight punch to your face level. Pull your left hand to your right shoulder, hand open, and cock your hips to the right. Snap your hips to the left and strike into his forearm with the sword edge of your left hand. Drop your palm onto his forearm, bending your wrist and draping your hand over his arm, pressing downward. Circle your hand over his forearm in a counterclockwise motion and pull his arm to your right, quickly grasping his right wrist with your right hand. This technique must be done quickly and requires practice.

This may also be done with the opposite (reverse) hand. When he punches with the right hand slide your left leg to your left forward and strike with a right sword hand into his forearm. Drape the right hand over his right forearm, circling his forearm in a clockwise motion, then quickly pull his right arm to your left, grabbing his right wrist with your left hand.

Low Level Scoop Block — In a right Fighting stance with the hands in a mid level guard, the opponent attacks with a right low level front kick to your groin area. Lower your left arm, striking into the opponent's leg with a left low level sweep block, hand open into a sword hand. Quickly turn the hand so that the top of the fingers (back of the hand) goes under the leg, the wrist bent upward in a hooking motion, palm downward. Rotate the left arm in a clockwise motion upward, trapping the leg between your forearm and your bicep.

The variation is for him to attack your groin area with a left front kick. Step the left foot to the right rear and lower the right arm. Hook the hand by bending the wrist backward, palm facing downward, and strike with the top of the forearm into his kicking leg after you have sidestepped the kick. As soon as your hand goes under the kick bring it upward in a clockwise rotation, trapping his leg between your bicep and forearm.

Evasion

It is often more useful to be able to evade blows than it is to block them. If you can slip a blow without having to take a backward step you may cause your opponent to off-balance himself and at the same time remain in striking range of him, able to take full advantage of his predicament. This may be used as a secondary method of avoiding being hit, or in conjunction with blocks.

To begin, when you assume a stance, keep your head and upper body relaxed. Stay alert, with your eyes on the opponent's solar plexus. Pay attention to his movements and to his range. You will need a training partner to practice this.

The Slip — Have your training partner stand in front of you in a Fighting stance. He takes a right lead and attacks your face with a right straight punch, at medium speed so that you see the punch and have a chance to avoid it. Shift your head and shoulders to the left just enough to avoid the punch. You may combine this with the left high level palm fist block for total efficiency. Freeze the action at this point and observe where your opponent is in relation to you. Look for the options you have in counterattacking.

Have him rechamber his right arm and attack you with a left straight reverse punch. Slip this punch by shifting your head and shoulders to the right, using a right palm fist high level block to ensure that you are not struck.

Have him rechamber his left arm and punch at your solar plexus with his right lead fist. Turn your torso to the right to avoid his punch, using the hips for an axis. You may combine this with the mid level palm fist block if you wish. When he rechambers his right fist, have him attack you with his left fist to your solar plexus. Turn your torso to the left to avoid this punch, using the mid level palm fist block if you wish. When slipping a blow, turn or move just enough to avoid the strike; do not exaggerate the movement. Angular movement is also helpful in evading blows.

The Dip — With your training partner in front of you in a Fighting stance, have him attack your high level with a right hook punch at slow or medium speed. The dip is done by bending your knees. Do not bend forward at the waist. If you do, you may expose yourself to a knee kick by the opponent. Do not lower your head forward as though nodding because you will lose sight of your opponent's hands and he may initiate a downward strike with the other hand, catching you in the side of the head. Bend the knees of both legs and dip under his strike, then spring up and forward into the opponent in counterattack. The dip works best against circular or arcing strikes, but it may be used against straight punches as well. You may also choose to use a rising forearm block or an outer deflection block with the dip to ensure that you successfully evade the blow.

Training for Blocking

To ensure that you are able to perform blocking techniques quickly and without having to pause to think about which method is appropriate in any given situation, you must train in many different situations to prepare yourself. While shadow combat is acceptable, where you perform the various techniques in different stances by yourself, nothing can take the place of a training partner attacking you so that you can see real strikes and kicks coming at you and evade or block them.

Prearranged Walking Blocks — You and your training partner stand facing each other at arm's length in left Fighting stances. Prior to the exercise you must have agreed on the three techniques he is about to attack you with. To begin, use only hand attacks at medium speed. For this example, we will use punches.

(1) He attacks your high level with a straight left punch. You shift into a right Back stance and block with a right outer deflection block. He then slides his left foot forward into a left Front stance and attacks your mid level with a right punch. You step backward into a right Front stance and block with a left mid level inner deflection block. He then uses the drag step method to slide the left foot forward and attacks your high level with a left hook punch. You dip under the hook punch and immediately step forward with the left foot forming a left Fighting stance and attack his high level with a left punch while he shifts into a right Back stance and blocks with a right outer deflection block. The rest of your attack and his blocks should mirror your blocks and his earlier attacks. Perform this set five times each as defenders.

(2) He attacks you with a right overhead hammer fist strike, stepping forward into a right Front stance. You slide the left foot to your left forward and block with a left rising forearm block. He then attacks you with a left reverse spear hand thrust to your mid level. You block with a right mid level inner deflection block. He then attacks with a left reverse sword hand blow to your high level. You block with a left

outer forearm block, then step forward with the right foot as he steps backward with his left foot, and attack him with a right overhead hammer fist. Proceed as in set one, performing the set four more times as a defender.

Vary the hand attacks to include all of them in the system in combination. This will help the attacker work on his hand combinations and the defender to block varied offenses. Select the appropriate block for each defensive move and try to work through all of the blocking techniques. When you have worked through the hand techniques, begin three attack combinations with kicks included; a hand attack first, then a kick, and then another hand attack. Vary this also, working through all of the kicks, using them as the opening attack as well. Begin working on angular movement to aid blocks and evasion methods.

Free Style Blocking — This is similar to the Walking blocks, but it allows the attacker to choose his own attack at will. There is no prearrangement. He attacks at medium speed at any level with any techniques that he chooses. However, he must attack in combinations of at least two attacks.

To begin, the two of you stand facing each other in Ready stances at arm's length. He steps forward into a right Fighting stance and attacks with a technique of choice. You may step in any direction that you choose, and use any stance and blocking method you feel is appropriate. He should attack you continuously for three minutes and then change roles, with you attacking him for three minutes.

Power Blocking — Building powerful and effective blocking power is a matter of body mechanics. This training method allows you to feel the power of a block in slow motion, as well as building it at the same time.

Assume a right Fighting stance and perform ten of each block with your right arm. As you perform them, have your training partner push against your blocking arm with just enough pressure to make you strain hard to complete the technique. Perform all of the blocks of the system on each arm in this manner, shifting from a right stance to a left stance when you change arms.

If you do not have a training partner or you cannot work out with him as often as you would like, there is an alternative exercise that builds strong blocks. Stand in a right Fighting stance and perform ten of each block with your right arm. As you perform them, tense all of the muscles involved as though you were pushing against a heavy weight. Do this to a slow ten count, exhaling as you perform the block.

In both exercises, rotate the hip of the blocking arm slowly with the block.

Falling

Learning the proper methods of falling will keep you from serious injury in the event you are tripped, thrown, or pushed to the ground. It will allow you to rebound from a seeming position of disadvantage quickly, so that the opponent does not have time to gain the advantage.

Back Fall — Begin in a crouch with the feet parallel. Pull both hands to the opposite shoulders in front of you, hands open and the palms turned inward. Extend one leg straight in front of you, and tuck your chin into your chest, rolling backward, staying round. Do not just fall flat onto your back. When the small of your back touches the ground, bring both arms down and slap the ground hard with the inside of the palms. This will help absorb the impact of the fall. Let the arms rebound from the ground and recross them over your chest.

When you have practiced this from a crouch and have the timing of the slap perfected, stand in a Ready stance with the hands crossed over your chest. Extend one leg in front of you and lower yourself on the other, tucking your head forward. Roll backward onto your back and slap the ground, exhaling as you slap.

Side Fall — Begin in a crouch with your hands crossed in front of your chest. Extend your right leg to your center line, or slightly to the left of it and roll backward onto your right hip. Slap the ground with the right hand and let it rebound.

Stand in a Ready stance and cross the arms over the chest. Extend your right leg slightly to the left, lowering yourself on the left leg, tuck your chin into your chest, and roll backward on the right hip. Slap the ground with the right hand, exhaling as you do so, and let the hand rebound from the ground. Stay round as you fall.

Perform this on both the right and left sides equally, as most throws may be performed with the right or left sides.

Front Fall — Kneel on the floor with your feet beneath you and your hands on your thighs. Fall forward from this position. Bring your hands up from your thighs, arms bent at the elbows, so that the palms and the forearms slap the floor as you fall forward, and not the elbows.

Stand in a Ready stance with your hands at your sides and fall straight forward without bending your knees. Bring your hands and forearms up from your sides so that they catch your fall without striking the elbows. Exhale as you do this.

You may use this method to break a fall while standing also. For example, if you are pushed from behind toward a solid object such as a wall, catch yourself with your hands and forearms against the wall, and rebound from it.

Forward Rolling Fall — Kneel on one knee with the other knee extended in front of you. Extend the arm on the side of the extended knee forward and place the hand just forward of the foot, near the big toe. Turn the hand so that the little finger touches the floor, the palm of the hand facing the foot. Push yourself forward, tucking your chin down into your chest and arching your back to stay as round as you can, and roll forward along the sword edge of your hand, onto your forearm, over your shoulder and in a diagonal line to the opposite hip. Perform a side fall.

Next, stand in a Ready stance. Step forward with the right foot and place the right hand down, just inside and slightly forward of the right foot with the little finger touching the ground first, palm facing the right foot. Tuck your chin down and arch your back, then roll forward down the forearm and diagonally across your back. Perform a left side fall.

When you have gained some proficiency at this, flip yourself in the air using this break-fall method. It should be practiced equally on both sides so that no matter what position you fall from you are able to effectively break your fall. Just at the moment of impact, exhale sharply. This will lock part of your breath in your lungs so that no matter how great the impact, it will not be knocked out of you. Before you learn throwing technique it is best to learn to fall properly.

You do not need mats for this, but a solid floor is hard and continued practice may dictate some type of cushioning be used. Several inches of carpet padding covered by one layer of carpet should be sufficient. Gymnastic mats are better if you can afford one for practice.

Grappling

For combative situations the use of foot sweeps, reaping throws, and other takedowns will often be an asset in closing the gap between you and the opponent or quickly taking him to the ground. Most throws may be used only for defense, after the opponent has attacked you and closed the gap, but sweeps may be used offensively and this is their prime value. Even if you do not take the opponent down you will break his balance and put yourself in position to finish the fight quickly. Throws are also useful for subduing an opponent that you may not wish to strike or kick.

All of the training situations described below begin with you and your opponent or training partner standing in front of each other at arms' length in left Fighting stances with your hands in the mid level guard.

Hooking Foot Sweep — *Defense:* He attacks you with a straight right punch to your high level. Step your right foot to your left rear forming a front facing Straddle stance and block with a left high level inner deflection block. Bring your left foot forward and hook the arch of your left foot behind his right heel, keeping it as close to the floor as you can. Do not go higher than mid-calf in actual combat for this sweep. The lower on his leg you can take him, the more leverage you will have for the throw. Now, sweep his right foot strongly to your right rear, dropping him onto his back. Follow up with a kick or hand attack.

Offense: Attack him with a high level left straight punch or spear hand to the eyes. Simultaneously, bring the right foot to the left in the foot replacement method. As he reacts to your first attack, arc your left foot to your right front, hooking your left foot's arch behind his left heel. Sweep strongly to your right rear, sweeping his left foot out from under him. When he falls, follow up with a kick or hand attack.

Side Foot Sweep — *Defense:* He attacks with a straight right punch to your high level. Block with a left outer forearm block. Swing the right foot forward in an arc until the arch of the right foot hooks the ankle of the opponent's left foot. In one fluid motion sweep the left foot of the opponent to your straight left, taking him down.

Offense: You attack his high level with a left across the body backfist and simultaneously move the right foot to the left using the foot replacement method. Sweep the left foot forward and to the left, hooking the ankle of the opponent's left foot with the arch of your left foot. Sweep his foot strongly to your straight right, taking his leg out from under him. He will fall face first to your left rear. Perform a follow up strike quickly.

Major Outer Reap — This is essentially the same in offense or defense; you must close the gap to use it.

Defense: Your opponent attacks with a right hook punch to your high level. Step your left foot to your left front and simultaneously block with an outer forearm block. Attack his chin with a rising palm fist strike. Bring your right leg to the left front in a circular motion, kicking it forward as though performing a rising kick. Then reap it backward, bent at the knee, so that the upper part of your rear thigh hooks the upper part of his inner thigh, and take his leg out from under him. As you reap his leg, drive it up as high as you can behind you, increasing the force of the reap. Push him to his right rear with your right hand under his chin, driving him head first into the ground. Follow

Side Foot Sweep
(1) Opponent begins attack, you parry

(2) Pull his arm and sweep his foot

(3) When he is down use a finishing punch

Major Outer Reap
(1) Fighting stance

(2) Opponent attacks with lunge punch, you use high level inner deflection, attack with palm fist thrust, grasp jacket/shirt

(3) Hook your right leg behind his right leg, reap leg out.

(4) Finish him

him down and perform a quick finishing technique.

Offense: Slide your left leg forward to the left front and attack the opponent with a left spear hand to the eyes. As he reacts to that, attack his neck with a right inward sword hand, dropping the left hand to cover or grasp his right hand. Swing the right leg around to the left front and swing it forward as though performing a rising kick. Reap it backward, taking his leg out from under him and thrusting him to his right rear with your right hand on his throat. Follow him down and perform a finishing technique.

Major Inner Reap — This also is much like the outer reap in that you must close the gap before you may use it.

Defense: He attacks with a low level right front snap kick. You slide forward with the left foot into a left Front stance and block his kick with a left low level scoop block. Bring the right leg straight forward, then to your right, hooking your right calf behind his left calf. Reap his left leg strongly to your right rear while retaining your hold on his right leg. He will fall hard on his upper back and head.

Offense: Attack him with a low level front kick with the right leg. Follow that quickly with a right straight thrust to his eyes. Set the right foot down inside his left leg and hook your right calf behind his left calf. Reap his left leg strongly to your right rear. As you reap his leg out from under him, attack his high level with a left palm thrust.

Rear Body Drop — *Defense:* He attacks with a right mid level side kick. Slide your left foot to your left front and block with a right low level sweep block so that the kick passes your right side. Bring the right leg in an arc to your left front, then set it down behind your opponent's legs, close to them. Encircle your opponent's leg with your right arm. Thrust your right hip to your right and pull his right hip close to your hip. Bend your knees and lower your center of gravity, and rotate the right foot onto the ball so that the heel faces to the right away from you. Snap your hips to the left pulling him over your right leg and hip. As you feel him go over, straighten the right leg with a snap. Drive him down onto the back of his head, drop to your knees and finish him.

Offense: Reach out with your left hand quickly, and grasp his right wrist. Pull it sharply to your left rear, and step the right foot to your right forward. Bring your left foot to your right forward, then over, behind both of his legs. Strike his throat or chin with a left arc hand strike, pivoting the left foot onto the ball so that the heel faces away from you, and snap your hips to the right, driving him over your left hip and leg. Drop to your knees and finish him.

Forward Body Drop — To perform this you must turn your back,

Major Inner Reap Against Round Kick
(1) Fighting stance

(2) He attacks with right leg round kick. Block should be left low level scoop block

(3) Trap his right leg with left arm in scoop block, hook your right leg behind his left, attack with palm fist

(4) Reap leg, finish him

(5) Resume fighting stance if faced with other opponents.

briefly, on the opponent, so it is best to have struck and stunned him first.

Defense: Your opponent attacks with a right high level hook punch. You step the left foot straight forward and block with a left outer forearm block, then grasp his right arm with your left hand, pulling his arm straight right. Strike him in the chin or throat with a right thrust, and step the right foot to your left forward, across the front of his legs. Pivot on the ball of the left foot 180 degrees counterclockwise, encircling his neck with the right arm and pulling with the left arm; with a sharp snap of the hips throw him over your right hip. Finish him quickly.

Offense: Attack his low level with a right front snap kick, and place the foot to your left front when you rechamber it. Attack his high level with a right hook punch as you set the foot down. Encircle his neck and pivot on the ball of the left foot 180 degrees counterclockwise, pulling him onto your right hip. With a sharp snap of the hips throw him onto his head over your right hip and leg. Drop to your knees and finish him.

Shoulder Throw — *Defense:* He attacks with a right overhead hammer fist. Step the right foot to your left front, just inside his right foot, and block with a left rising forearm block. Turn into a right Straddle stance and attack his midsection with a right inverted fist or spear hand, grasping his right arm with your left hand as you strike. Step the left foot to your right front, inside his left foot, so that your feet are approximately parallel, pivoting 180 degrees counterclockwise so that your back is to him and you are in a front facing Straddle stance. As you pivot, either encircle his neck with your right arm from the right side so that his head is over your shoulder, or hook the right elbow under his right armpit so that your forearm is behind his right shoulder. Bend both knees and pull him onto your right hip. Snap the hips sharply to the right and straighten both knees, throwing him over your right hip and shoulder. If you have encircled his neck you may break it throwing him this way.

Throws should be learned on both sides so that you are able to perform them with either leg in any situation as required. They are effective methods of taking the opponent off his feet, many times by surprise.

Low Kicks

When you have taken the opponent to the ground and he is still hostile, willing to continue the fight, you should not surrender your control over the situation by allowing him to regain his feet. Low kicks are the one way to ensure that he does not.

Forward Heel Kick — With your training partner prone at your feet, head to the left and feet to the right, chamber the right leg as though for a right front kick. Pivot on the ball of the left foot to face your left front and attack his solar plexus, chin, or face by snapping the right leg downward. Cock the toes and the foot up so that the bottom rear of the heel strikes the opponent, driving inward and slightly upward.

Side Kick — This is performed in the same manner that a regular side snap kick is performed. With the opponent down, chamber the leg for a side kick. Snap the hip into it first, then strike to the target with the sword edge of the foot, leaning into the kick slightly.

Outside Crescent Kick — With the opponent at your feet, head to your left and feet to your right, raise the right foot into a right outside crescent kick as high as you can. Stop the kick at your own center line and drop it straight down into the opponent's body, striking with the rear of the heel.

Inside Crescent Kick — This is the exact opposite of an outside crescent kick to the low level. These are very powerful kicking methods.

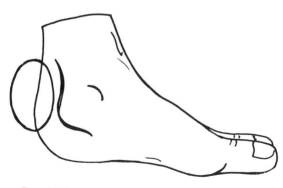

Rear heel

Finishing Technique

If you have dazed and thrown the opponent, you may choose to follow him to the ground by bending your knees rather than standing up and kicking him. If so, you still must stop him from continuing the fight by striking him.

Low Level Punch — With your training partner at your feet in front of you, head to your left and feet to your right, drop to your right knee, leaving the left knee extended. Pull your right fist to the guard position, rotate your right hip forward, striking downward into him. In a dropping movement, use the momentum of the drop to add power to the strike.

Most of the striking technique may be applied in this manner, the sword hand and hammer fist blows being the most practical.

Chapter Six

Defense

This action is broken up into specific sets that you may use as a base for understanding self-defense as it applies to real fights. Begin slowly so that you understand the techniques and the sequences, and do not injure your training partner. As your skill increases the control of your technique, improve your speed and reflexes when performing these self-defense sets. Use full power but stop the blow just short of impact. To make this realistic, your training partner should go with your technique, as though your blows really were landing. For example, if you kick him in the stomach, he should bend forward as though he really had just been kicked in the stomach. This is very important.

Since there are no "control" techniques such as arm bars or wrist locks in this system, the emphasis is on fighting. The situations described are meant to be a prelude to violence on the aggressor's part, he having made it clear to you that he is not satisfied to merely talk, but plans physical harm to you. Therefore the sets listed below are not always performed when you are confronted, but only after you are sure you are acting in defense of yourself or others.

Wrist Grab — Your training partner grabs your right wrist with his left hand as you both stand in Ready stances.

(1) A grab of this nature is often a prelude to a fist attack with his other hand. Step your right foot to your right front forming an Angular stance and attack his bladder or solar plexus with a left round kick. Follow it quickly with a left palm fist thrust to his chin or nose.

(2) Step the right foot straight forward forming a right Fighting stance and attack his groin with a left front snap kick. Follow it quickly with a left downward elbow strike to the back of his head.

(3) Step the left foot to your right front and strike into his left forearm with a left palm fist thrust, freeing your right arm. Pivot on the ball of the left foot 180 degrees and attack his bladder with a spin right back thrust kick.

This time your training partner grabs your right hand with his right hand as you both stand in Ready stances.

(1) Step your left foot to your left forward and attack his high level with a left hook punch. Step the right leg around his right leg, grasp him with your right hand and reap his right leg out from under him with a major outer reap.

(2) Slide your right foot straight right and attack his high level with a left arc hand. Sweep his right or both legs out from under him with a left side foot sweep.

(3) Circle his right wrist with your right hand counterclockwise, grasping it firmly with the thumb below the four fingers around his inner forearm. Step the right foot to the straight rear and pull his right arm to you. Strike into his extended right elbow with a left palm fist thrust and break it.

Lapel Grabs — Your training partner grabs your shirt at chest level with his left hand, pulling you to him slightly, and cocks the right fist for a strike.

(1) As he pulls you in, use the momentum he creates. Drive a left straight thrust with the fist or palm fist into his mid level, stepping forward with the left foot. If he punches after the strike, block with an outer forearm block with the left hand as you retract it from the thrust. Bring the right foot in and take him down with an inner reaping throw.

(2) As he grabs you, strike into his left arm with a right downward elbow strike, knocking his arm away. From the elbow strike, hit him across the bridge of the nose with an across the body sword hand strike, stepping forward with the right foot and forming a right Straddle stance. Encircle his neck with the right arm, step the right foot to your left front, bring the left foot to your right front and throw him over your right hip with a forward body drop throw.

(3) Block the punch after he has grabbed you with a left outer parry, and strike into the elbow of his left arm with a right rising block, stepping the right foot forward into a right Front stance. Hit him in the solar plexus with a left inverted fist, cocking the right arm and delivering a right outside sword hand to his neck.

This time your training partner steps forward with his left foot and grabs your shirt at chest level with both hands, pushing you backward.

(1) Step backward with your right foot and attack his right elbow with a left palm fist hook strike, knocking both of his arms away from you. Pivot on the ball of the right foot and deliver a left side thrust kick to his lead knee. Set the foot down forming a left Front stance and attack his midsection with a right front thrust kick.

(2) Dip below his hands as he reaches to grab you, stepping the left foot forward into a left Fighting stance. Knee kick him in the midsection with a right knee kick. Rechamber the leg, and attack his inner left knee with a right side thrust kick, knocking him down.

(3) As he reaches to grab you, attack both of his arms with a right outside crescent kick, knocking both arms away from you. Set the

right foot down to your left front, pivot counterclockwise on the ball of the right foot, and deliver a left spin back thrust kick to his midsection. Set the left foot down straight forward into a left Straddle stance and attack his high level with a left across the body sword hand.

Forward Push — Your training partner steps forward and pushes you backward with his right hand in your chest. This is often a prelude to a rushing attack where he rushes in on you while you are off balance; or he waits for you to recover and step in toward him and he is ready for you.

(1) Step backward with the left foot forming a left Back stance and parry his push with a left outer deflection, simultaneously attacking his high level with a right lead punch. Attack his outer right thigh with a left round kick. Place the arch of your left foot behind his right knee and thrust downward, taking him to his knees and attack the side of his head with a right across the body hammer fist.

(2) Step your right foot to your right front parrying his pushing arm with a right high level inner deflection block. Attack his mid level with a left spear hand thrust. As he bends forward from the spear hand, shift from a right Front stance to an Angular stance and strike his high level with a right across the body backfist.

(3) As he steps forward to push you, step the left foot forward forming a right Back stance and block his push with a left outer forearm block. Strike the side of his head with a right outside sword hand and grab his hair. Pull his head downward sharply and knee kick him in the forehead with your right knee. Place the right foot on the inside of his right knee and thrust it away from you strongly, taking him down.

Your training partner reaches for you with both hands this time, pushing you in the chest with both palms.

(1) As he steps forward to push you, thrust kick him in the midsection with a right front thrust kick. Set the right foot forward forming a right Front stance. Strike his high level with a right punch, drop your hand to his left shoulder and pull him to you. Attack his high level with a left arc hand.

(2) Step your left foot straight left forming an Angular stance and block into his arms with a right outer forearm block. Attack the right side of his neck with a left middle single knuckle fist strike. Swing the right leg up and around behind his right leg, grab his right shoulder with your right hand, and reap his leg out from under him, taking him down. Drop and finish him with a right downward punch.

(3) When his arms come forward to push, block both hands with two simultaneous outer deflections. Kick him in the groin with a right

front snap kick. Set the foot down forward and attack his chin with a right rising elbow strike.

The push comes from the rear this time. The opponent standing behind you and stepping forward pushes you in the upper back with both hands.

(1) When he pushes you, take one step forward with the right foot and perform a forward rolling fall, coming to your feet and turning to face him at the end of the roll. Perform this technique if you do not see or hear the attacker before he is on you.

(2) You see or hear the attacker as he approaches. Turn and look over your left shoulder so you have a target. Attack his midsection with a left rear thrust kick. Set the foot down to your straight rear forming a left Straddle stance and attack his high level with a left across the body hammer fist.

(3) Again you hear or see the attacker before he is on you. Step the right foot to your left front forming a right Back stance, facing him at an angle. Attack his high level with a left arc hand. Attack his high level with a right punch just after the arc hand. Chamber the right leg and kick into the side of the knee of the lead leg, taking him down.

Two Hand Front Choke — This happens in a fight from time to time when the opponent closes the gap and is in a killing rage. You must first relieve the pressure of the choke before you stop him from choking you again.

(1) Your training partner grabs your windpipe with both hands and tightens his fingers enough for you to feel pressure. Drive both palm fists upward into his elbows simultaneously, knocking his fingers away from your throat. Kick him in the groin with a right front snap kick. Set the right foot to your right rear forming a left Front stance. As the opponent bends forward from the groin kick, kick him in the face with another right front snap kick, using the ball of the foot this time.

(2) He grabs you again in the same manner. Step the left foot to the straight rear forming a right Straddle stance. Attack his forearms with a right outside hammer fist strike, knocking his hands off your throat and to the left. Bring the right hand to the left shoulder and strike his high level with a right across the body backfist. Chamber the right leg and kick his midsection with a right side snap kick.

(3) As his hands go up for your throat, lunge forward with a left across the body backfist to his face, stepping the left foot straight forward forming a left Front stance. Quickly drive your right knee into his groin, then set the right foot down to your left rear and strike into the back of his head with a right downward across the body hammer fist.

Rear Choke Hold — Your training partner wraps his right arm around your throat from behind, the crook of his elbow centered on your windpipe. His left arm goes over your left shoulder, the palm of his left hand is placed against the back of your head; the palm of his right hand is placed in the crook of the left elbow for leverage. This is often called the Sleeper Choke Hold. It restricts the air to the brain by cutting off the blood supply in the carotid and jugular. It applies pressure to the side of your neck. A variation is to place the right forearm across the windpipe; the hand positioning is the same. This is more dangerous and should not be practiced until you can defend against the Sleeper first. Your first priority is to relieve the pressure of the choke hold.

(1) As soon as the choke is applied, step the right foot to the right and drive your left elbow backward into the opponent's solar plexus. Strike hard into his groin with a left palm slap. Step your left foot to your right rear, circling your foot behind his right leg and strike into his right eye with a right spear hand hook strike. Sweep his right leg out from under him with a left side foot sweep, taking him down. Drop beside him and finish him with a downward strike.

(2) When you feel the pressure of his arm around your throat, turn your left shoulder slightly to the right rear and stomp your left foot down onto his right instep, back of the heel striking first. Chamber the left leg and attack his groin with a rear snap kick. Set the left foot down between his feet; step the right foot straight forward forming a left Straddle stance and drive a left side elbow strike into his temple.

(3) When he has you in the choke, turn the left shoulder to the rear slightly and drive the left elbow into his solar plexus. Rotate quickly and drive the right elbow into his right ribs, grasping his right arm with your left hand as you strike. Reach up and grasp his right arm with your right hand also. Step the right foot to the straight right and throw him over your right leg and hip with a forward body drop throw. Chamber the right leg and attack his head with a low level heel kick.

These are common defenses against encounters on the street where the opponent is close enough to grab you. To get that close, he must not broadcast his intention to attack until he is making his move. You must react quickly to this form of attack since his initial move is usually a set up for a strike or even an armed attack. These should be practiced on both sides (left side and right, one side being the mirror of the other when performing the sets), so that no matter what direction the opponent attacks from, you are ready for him.

The next set of defenses are against unarmed opponents when they come at you from the front, having broadcast their intent beforehand. Normally, they will attack you in a straight line, trying to punch you as soon as they are close enough. You must not allow them to close the gap for this "sucker punch" in the first place; be alert to their movements. When they attack, counterattack quickly and end the fight.

Roundhouse Punch — Your training partner attacks you with a punch which begins with him drawing his right hand back behind him and swinging in a large looping motion at your head. You begin in a Ready stance or a Natural Forward stance. As he punches he steps forward with the left foot. This is often used as a surprise attack in street encounters, and is also used in combat. It is not economical of motion and is easily stopped.

(1) As he steps forward and starts the swing, you step the left foot straight forward and block into his right arm with a left outer forearm block, forming a left Front stance. Attack his midsection with a right straight punch, withdrawing the left hand to the guard. Step straight forward with the right foot, forming a right Front stance, attacking with a right lunge punch to his high level. Swing the right foot in behind his left foot and take him down with an inner reaping throw.

(2) As he swings, dip below the punch, sliding the left foot forward forming a left Fighting stance, and strike him in the midsection with a right hook punch. As you straighten up, strike his high level with a left hook punch. Grasp his right shoulder and pull him toward you with your left hand, attacking his chin with a rising right elbow strike, shifting into a left Front stance.

(3) When he winds up for the punch, step forward with your right foot and attack his low section with a left front snap kick. Strike his neck or collar bones with a right downward sword hand as you set the left foot forward into a left Fighting stance. Strike into his chin or throat area from below with a left inverted fist strike.

Straight Right Reverse Punch — The opponent stands in a left Fighting stance and attacks with a straight right punch to your high level. This is used often as a sucker punch or a first strike technique because for a right-handed person it is his strongest strike. You begin in a Ready stance.

(1) As he punches you, step the left foot forward forming a right Back stance and block the punch with a left rising block. Attack with a right single middle knuckle fist punch to his mid level as you shift into a left Front stance. Hit him in the high level with a left hook punch. Chamber the left leg and attack the inside of his left knee with a left front snap kick.

(2) As he punches, step the left foot to the left forward, slipping

the punch, and blocking it with a right outer forearm block, shifting into an Angular stance. Strike his high level with a left punch. Strike his groin with a right upward arc hand, pulling your left hand to the right shoulder. Strike into his high level with a left across the body sword hand.

(3) When he steps forward with the left foot to begin the punch, pivot on the ball of the left foot and deliver a right snap side kick into his mid level. Step the right foot straight forward forming a right Straddle stance and deliver a right across the body backfist strike to his high level. Hook your right leg behind his left leg and reap his leg out from under him with an inner reaping throw.

Straight Lead Left Jab — The opponent steps forward with the left foot and attacks your face with a straight left punch. This is often the opening move of a fight where the opponent uses this to attract your attention before he launches a right reverse punch to finish the fight. Interrupt his timing and stop him from using the right hand.

(1) As he punches, step your right foot to your right front, slipping the punch, bringing the right hand up in a high level inner deflection block. Attack his midsection with a left round kick. Set the left foot down to your left front forming a left Fighting stance and attack the back of his head with a left across the body sword hand. Hook the left foot arch into the front of the opponent's left ankle and sweep his foot out from under him backward with a side foot sweep, dropping him onto his face.

(2) As he jabs, dip below it stepping the left foot straight forward forming a left Fighting stance, and as you straighten up attack with a right punch to his high level. Attack his high level with a left arc hand. Attack his groin with a right knee kick, then kick into the inside of his left knee with a right side thrust kick, taking him down.

(3) When he steps forward to punch, step the left foot straight forward and block with a left high level inner deflection as you form a right Back stance. Shift into a left Front stance and attack the side of his neck with a left across the body sword hand. Attack his mid level with a right front thrust kick, setting the foot down forward forming a right Front stance. The thrust kick should knock him backward. Using the foot replacement method bring the left foot to the right and attack with a right angle thrust kick to his midsection.

Left-Right Combination — The opponent steps forward with his left foot and attacks your face with a left lead punch and then a right reverse punch. This is the standard attack in most fights.

(1) The opponent steps forward and attacks with the left lead punch and you step your left foot straight forward forming a left Fighting

stance. Block his jab with a right outer deflection block. Attack his high level with a straight left punch. This may cause him not to punch with his right hand, especially if you catch him stepping forward to throw the right. In this case have him attack with the right punch after you punch with the left hand. As you retract the left from the punch he attacks with the right. Block with your left hand using an outer forearm block. Attack with a right hook punch to his high level and follow it up with a right low level front snap kick.

(2) As he punches with the left hand, step back with the left foot forming a left Back stance. Block with a right outer forearm block. He attacks immediately with his right hand, lunging toward you now, since you have stepped back. As he punches kick him in the mid level with a left front snap kick, blocking his punch with a right high level inner deflection block. Set the left foot down forward forming a left Front stance and attack his high level with a left palm fist thrust. Follow him backward with a right lunge punch forming a right Front stance, striking to his high level.

(3) As he jabs, slip your head to the right and block with a high level inner deflection with the right hand. Lunge forward with the left foot forming a left Front stance and striking him in the throat with a left spear hand. Step the right foot to the right front forming a right Front stance and attack the back of his head with a right outer sword hand, pivoting into an Angular stance. Do not give him the chance to attack with the right hand.

Hook Punch — The opponent steps forward with the left foot and attacks the high level with a left hook punch. This is often seen as a sucker punch, or the initial attack in a confrontation. It is often used at the end of a two punch combination or off a jab lead. The hook punch can be deceptive and comes in from what can be a blind angle, so be alert for it.

(1) As the punch is thrown, slide your left foot straight forward forming a left Fighting stance and block with a right outer forearm block into his left bicep. Attack his chin with a left inverted punch. Attack his face with a right outer backfist off the block. Reach up with both hands and grasp his head, pulling it forward and downward sharply, and drive your right knee upward into his face.

(2) As he hooks, dip below it, sliding the right foot to the right front, and attack his bladder with a left round kick. Rechamber the leg without setting it down and kick into his face with a left round kick as he leans forward from the force of the first round kick. Set the left foot down to your left rear forming a right Fighting stance, and chamber an across the body hammer fist. Pivot into an Angular stance

and deliver the across the body hammer fist with the left hand to the back of his head.

(3) The opponent attacks to your mid level with his left hook punch. Drive your right elbow back and down into his left forearm, blocking the punch. Strike to his high level with a straight left punch, stepping the left foot forward forming a left Fighting stance. Follow immediately with a right straight punch to his high level, then a left hook punch to the high level.

Uppercut — The opponent steps in close to you, and attacks with a right uppercut (a rising inverted fist punch) to your high level, his left foot forward.

(1) As he punches, step your right foot straight back forming a right Back stance. Block with a right mid level inner deflection block, pushing the attacker's forearm to your left, away from your body. Grab his right wrist with your left hand and attack his throat with a right across the body sword hand. Attack his mid level with a left inverted fist punch, chambering the right arm as you strike, and deliver a right side elbow strike into the side of his head as he leans forward from the inverted fist strike.

(2) As he punches, step forward with the left foot and strike into his right forearm with a left palm fist thrust, driving his uppercut back into him. Attack his high level with a right lateral elbow strike. Attack his high level with a left hook punch. Drive a right upward elbow strike into his high level to finish him.

(3) This time he attacks your mid level with the uppercut. As he steps forward to punch, block with a forward elbow block. Rather than bringing it upward, hook the left elbow inward, striking it into his forearm. Step the left foot forward and perform a hooking foot sweep against his left foot. As he goes down, strike his high level with a left across the body backfist strike. Drop down and finish him.

Overhead Attack — The opponent steps forward with the right foot and attacks the top of your head with a right overhead attack, simulating a club attack. You may choose to arm your partner with a club, but it is best learned empty-handed first, so that you understand the timing of the block. Your target for the block is the arm and not the club. Use of the club too early may cause you to block the club itself.

(1) As he attacks with a right hammer fist strike, slide the left foot straight forward and block into his elbow with a left rising forearm block. This will cause his arm to snap straight, injuring his elbow, and may cause him to drop the club. Attack with a right front kick to his groin, setting the right foot forward to form a right Front stance. Attack with a right palm fist thrust to his high level. Attack his throat

with a left spear hand thrust.

(2) As he attacks, step the left foot to the right rear forming a right Straddle stance, slipping the strike but blocking into it with a left outer deflection block. Use the foot replacement method and bring the left foot to the right and attack his mid level with a right side snap kick. Set the right foot to your left front and attack with a spin rear thrust kick to his bladder area with the left leg. Set the left foot down straight forward and attack his high level with a left across the body backfist.

(3) As he steps forward to attack, kick him in the low level with a right front snap kick, then set the foot down to your right front. Block the attack with a left outer forearm block after the kick, as you form a right Front stance. Attack his high level with a right thrust punch. Drive a left knee kick into his groin and chamber the leg for a left side kick. Kick into the inner side of his right knee with your left leg using a side thrust kick, taking him down. Follow him down and finish the fight.

Front Kick — The opponent attacks your groin with a right front kick from a Ready stance.

(1) As the opponent kicks, step back with the right leg forming a right Back stance and block with a left low level palm fist block. As soon as his kick is deflected, attack his midsection with a right round kick. Set the right foot forward forming a right Front stance and attack the right side of his neck or right collar bone with a right across the body sword hand. Snap the right elbow upward and attack his chin with a right rising elbow strike. Follow it with a left palm fist thrust to his high level.

(2) As the opponent kicks, step back with the left leg forming a right Fighting stance and perform a left low level scoop block. Attack his high level with a right punch. Attack the back of his right thigh with a left knee kick, setting the left foot forward. Step the right leg forward and behind the opponent's supporting left leg and perform an inner reaping throw. Follow him down and finish the fight.

(3) As he chambers for the kick, deliver a right outside crescent kick to the inside of his right knee, knocking him off balance. Set the right foot down to your left front and attack his solar plexus with a right inverted fist punch. Encircle his neck with the right hand, step the left foot to your right front, and throw the opponent over your right leg and hip with a forward body drop throw. Finish the fight with a low level attack.

Side Kick — The opponent attacks your left knee by pivoting on the left foot and kicking with his right leg using a right side snap kick.

(1) As he kicks, step your left leg straight back forming a right

Fighting stance and block with a left low level sweep block. Grasp his ankle with your left hand, pulling it to you, and strike into his knee with your right palm fist, breaking his right knee. Use the foot replacement method and bring the left foot to the right, then attack his left knee with a right side snap kick, taking him down.

(2) As he kicks, attack his right leg with a left reverse crescent kick, knocking his kick aside. Set the left foot to your left forward and form a left Front stance. Attack his mid level with a right spear hand thrust. Attack the side of his head with a left outer hammer fist. Step the right foot forward forming a right Front stance and attack with a right lunge punch to his high level, finishing the fight.

(3) As he pivots, the kick chambered, lunge forward with the right foot and jam the knee of the left leg into his right thigh, jamming his kick. Hit him in the high level with a left punch, then a left across the body backfist. Follow it with a right straight punch to his high level.

Round Kick — The opponent steps forward with the right foot, attacking with a left round kick to your right outer thigh in the kickboxing style.

(1) As he kicks, step the right leg straight forward, jamming his kick even though it is already in the air. You will be inside it. Form a right Front stance and drive your right elbow downward into his upper thigh. From the elbow strike, punch with the right hand into his high level. Attack with a left knee kick into his groin. As he bends forward from the strike, attack the back of his head with a left downward elbow strike.

(2) As he kicks, attack his left lower leg with a left outside crescent kick, knocking his kick aside. Rechamber the kicking leg and attack his right supporting knee with a left side thrust kick. Step the left foot to your left front and set it down forming an Angular stance, attacking his high level with a left across the body backfist. Follow it immediately with a right straight punch to his high level.

(3) As he steps forward to chamber the kick, raise your right knee and thrust it into his left knee, knocking him off balance to his left. Set the right foot down to your right front and strike him in the side of the neck with a left arc hand. Attack his low section with a left knee kick, then set the left foot down where it was and attack his high level with a right palm fist thrust.

Outer Crescent Kick — The opponent steps forward with his left foot and attacks your high level with a right outside crescent kick. It is doubtful that you will find an attack of this nature unless you are fighting a martial artist, but it is better to be prepared than found wanting.

(1) As he kicks, step the right foot forward and block with a left outer forearm block. Grasp his leg with the left hand and strike him in the high level with an outer sword hand strike with the right hand. Slide your right leg behind his left leg and reap his left leg out from beneath him with an inner reaping throw.

(2) As he kicks, step the right foot to the right front forming a right Front stance and block the kick with a right high level inner deflection block. Strike his midsection with a left inverted fist punch. Bring your left leg up to the right and then attack his high level with a left reverse crescent kick.

(3) As he steps forward and prepares to kick, pivot on the ball of your left foot and attack his left knee with a right side kick. Let the foot down straight forward forming a right Straddle stance and attack his midsection with a right side elbow strike. Pull the right arm back across your body and attack his high level with a right across the body backfist. Attack his low level with a left front snap kick.

Inside Crescent Kick — The opponent steps forward with his right foot and attacks your high level with a reverse crescent kick with the left leg.

(1) As he kicks, step the left foot to your right front stepping inside his kick and effectively jamming it. Form a left Fighting stance and attack the right side of his neck with a left arc hand. Step the left foot behind his legs and take him over your left hip and leg in a rear body drop throw, pulling with the right hand on his left shoulder and your left hand at his throat. Follow him down and finish him.

(2) As he kicks, step your left foot to your straight right, in front of your right foot, and pivot on the ball of your left foot. Attack his midsection with a spin rear thrust kick with the right leg while his kick is still in the air. This will knock him down.

(3) As he kicks, step the left foot straight back forming a left Back stance, effectively slipping the kick, and block into it with the right forward elbow block. This will injure his lower leg and turn him slightly to his right. Step the left foot straight forward forming a left Front stance and attack his high section with a left lunge punch. Pull the left hand back and strike both ears with a double cupped palm strike. Grab his head and pull it downward as you knee kick upward with your right knee into his head.

Foot Sweep — Since the defense against both the hooking and the side foot sweeps are roughly the same, the side foot sweep is described as it is the more common of the two. You and your opponent stand facing each other in left Fighting stances and he attacks your lead left foot with a right side foot sweep.

(1) As he foot sweeps, lift your left foot and allow his sweep to pass underneath. As you lift it, chamber the left leg for a side kick and pivot on the ball of the right foot. Attack the knee of his sweeping leg as he stops the sweep motion. This should drive him to the floor on his right knee. Set your left foot to your left forward and attack his face with a right round kick, knocking him over onto his back. Set the right foot down straight forward and attack his head with a left heel kick.

(2) As he sweeps, step your left foot to the rear forming a right Straddle stance, letting the foot pass in front of you. As it passes, attack with a foot replacement right side snap kick to his midsection. Reach out with the right hand and grab his head, pulling it to you. Attack the right side of his head with a lateral forward elbow strike with the left arm. Cock the right arm and attack the right side of his head with an across the body right hammer fist.

(3) As he begins the sweep, lift the left leg and kick him in the midsection with a left front snap kick. Set the left foot down to your left front and attack him with a right downward sword hand as you form a left Front stance. Strike his left collar bone. Bring the right leg around behind his right leg and reap it out from under him using a major outer reaping throw. Follow him down and finish him.

Reaping Throw — The opponent steps close to you with his left foot to your right rear, and attempts a major outer reaping throw, his right hand grasping your lapel.

(1) As he begins the reap, step your left foot to your right rear, turning the opponent. Raise your right leg, pull his left shoulder to you with your left hand, and reap his right leg out from under him with your right leg, countering his attack.

(2) As he begins his reap, slide your right leg behind both of his legs and attack his chin with a rising palm fist strike with the right hand. Throw him over your right hip and leg with a reverse body drop throw.

(3) As he throws you, grasp his right arm with your left hand at the forearm, and grasp his lapel or left shoulder with your right hand. As you fall twist your hips sharply to your left, pulling his right shoulder downward and to your left with your left hand, and pushing to your left with your right hand. When you land continue this pressure, pulling him so that he trips over you and falls across your body on his head. Roll over on top of him and finish him.

Turning Throw — The opponent steps close to you and turns, attempting to throw you with a forward body drop throw, his right leg extended for the throw.

(1) As he begins the throw, drop forward onto your right knee so

that it lands on his bent right knee, slamming his knee into the floor. Reach over his right shoulder with your left hand and grasp his chin, pulling his head back and to your left. Pull him over your left knee and strike into his solar plexus with a right hammer fist.

(2) As he begins his throw, step your right leg over his right leg and place both of your hands on his right hip. Form an Angular stance and thrust downward with both of your hands pushing him down. Attack with a left knee kick into his spine.

(3) As he begins his throw, arch your back and turn your right hip into his right hip, moving close to his body, and pushing against him with both hands. Attack his coccyx with a left knee kick. This should stop his throw. Reach over his right shoulder with your left hand and pull his head backward, under your left armpit and strike into his solar plexus with your right hammer fist.

Chapter Seven

Holistic Training

A schedule for overall training is easily prepared, but it may not be as easy to follow due to time limitations or other activities. You may find yourself able to perform only parts of your workout at one time, breaking it into fragments during the day one time, and able to complete more than anticipated at others. The recommended regimen is to schedule enough time for yourself every day to do a short workout. Three times a week, or every other day, perform one full training session as they are outlined here, but try to fit some of the stretches and calisthenics or weight routines into your weekly activities. If you can keep up a workout three times weekly for six months you will notice a dramatic improvement in your health and in your martial abilities.

Below are listed eleven points that should be kept in mind as you train. They reflect the essence of training.

(1) Keep your mind on the moment, not letting it wander or be distracted by anything not directly related to your training.

(2) Learn to maintain good balance in your movement. Move smoothly and gracefully in training. Keep your center of balance low and stay relaxed. When you assume a stance keep both feet flat on the ground.

(3) Keep your movement fluid until the moment of impact with the target.

(4) Use your weight when you strike. Use of the proper body mechanics is essential and if you master it in training you will use it correctly in combat. Never try to out-muscle your opponent.

(5) Make your footwork fast and appropriate for the situation. Do not dance around just for the sake of movement. Excessive movement wastes time and effort.

(6) Always use proper breathing methods to generate power and to refresh yourself. Breathe *out* with tension and breathe *in* during relaxation.

(7) Keep your eyes and your attention on your opponent(s), but do not develop tunnel vision, blinding yourself to events around you.

(8) Make each movement appropriate to the situation. Do not attempt to carry through a technique or movement that is no longer useful. Combat is fluid and one technique may lead to another, but

183

if you attempt one and the opponent avoids it, go on to the next move that is required, not one that is simply programmed.

(9) Make the most of your training time by concentrating and working hard. Merely going through the motions is a waste of time, and you have none to spare!

(10) When you first learn a new technique have someone demonstrate it for you several times so that you can see how it works. Try it yourself on both sides. Then go over the exact movements so that you will be able to practice it correctly. Begin doing the technique slowly, then work to perfect it. A technique done strongly and correctly is worth ten times one done too fast and sloppily.

(11) Learn each new technique and stance equally on both sides so that you may apply them strongly with either the right or left, depending on the angle or number of attacks by your opponent(s).

Specific Training Methods

One Step Sparring — You stand at arm's length from your training partner both in Ready stances. The Attacker *(A)* steps forward with his right foot forming a right Fighting stance and attacks your high level with a right hand technique. Whatever technique you are learning is the one that *A* uses. You, the Defender *(D),* take one step either forward, backward, or at an angle into an appropriate stance, perform an appropriate block (the one you are learning during that session), and then quickly counterattack. *A* performs his technique and freezes. In the beginning the attack, stances, blocks and counterattacks are prearranged; that is, you and your training partner have agreed beforehand that he will attack with a certain technique to a specific area, and you will perform a specific counter. At advanced training levels, the defense is free form. Repeat this exercise with the attacker using his left side.

Two Step Sparring — *A* and *D* face each other at arms length in Ready stances. *A* then steps forward with his right foot forming a right Fighting stance and attacks *D's* high level with a right hand technique. *D* takes one step, forming an appropriate stance, and uses an appropriate block. *A* then attacks with a left side technique. *D* shifts stances, blocks and counterattacks. Return to Ready stances and repeat with *A* stepping forward with his left foot. This is prearranged at first.

Three Step Sparring — Same as above, but after the reverse side technique, *A* steps forward with his reverse side and attacks with a third technique. This is a driving attack. *D* may step in any direction and into any stance that is appropriate, using appropriate blocks as *A* chases him, but *D* does not counter until after the third attack from *A*. Repeat this starting with the left side. This is prearranged at first.

Four Step Sparring — *A* steps forward with his right foot and attacks *D's* high level with a right side technique. *D* steps and blocks. *A* then attacks with a left reverse technique. *D* steps and blocks. *A* then steps forward with his left foot and attacks with his left side. *A* attacks with a right reverse technique. *D* steps and blocks, then counterattacks. Return to Ready stances and repeat with *A* stepping out with his left side. This is prearranged at first.

Five Step Sparring — *A* steps forward with his right foot and attacks *D's* high level with a right side technique. *D* steps and blocks. *A* then attacks with a left side technique. *D* steps and blocks. *A* steps forward with the left foot and attacks *D* with a high level left technique. *D* steps and blocks. *A* attacks with a reverse right technique. *D* steps and blocks. Then *A* steps forward with his right foot and attacks with a right technique. *D* steps and blocks, then counterattacks.

The descriptions given are to start with. Three technique combinations may and should be used without the need for *A* to step forward during three, four and five step sparring. Kicks will take the place of some of the stepping also.

Free Form Blocking — *A* and *D* stand in Ready stances at arms length. *A* then attacks *D* with a series of techniques that *D* must evade, parry or block. This continues for three minutes at which time *A* and *D* return to the Ready stance. *D* then becomes the attacker, chasing the other man around with combinations for three minutes.

Training Schedule

Each session consists of a ninety-minute workout which may be broken up into segments for your convenience. It is recommended that you perform the last hour in consecutive segments though, and that you perform each segment without any interruptions.

1st Session:

15 minutes Stretching and Warm Up Exercises

15 minutes Stances and Footwork

30 minutes Basic Straight Punches and Heavy Bag
  Demonstration

15 minutes Basic Blocking and One Step Sparring
  Demonstration

15 minutes Basic Kicking and Heavy Bag Demonstration

Techniques:

Stances: Introduction to the Ready, Natural Forward, Fighting, Front and Back Stances

Footwork: Glide Step

Punches: Introduction to the Lunge, Reverse and Lead Punches

Blocks: High Level Sweep Block, Low Level Sweep Block, Rising Block

Kicks: Front, Side, Rear Kicks

2nd Session:

15 minutes Stretching and Warm Up Exercises

15 minutes Stances and Footwork

30 minutes Kicking and Heavy Bag Work

15 minutes Blocking in One and Two Step Sparring

15 minutes Straight Punches in Combination and Heavy Bag Work

Techniques:

Stances: Stance shifting with punches, blocks, and combinations

Footwork: Review Glide Step, introduce Drag Step, demonstrate the transitory nature of stances

Kicking: Concentrate on hard bag kicks and proper body mechanics

Blocking: Concentrate on proper body mechanics and timing the blocks in One and Two Step Sparring

Punching: 1-2-3 basic straight punch combinations on heavy bag; work for power

3rd Session:

15 minutes Stretching and Warm Up Exercises

15 minutes Stances and Footwork

30 minutes Blocks in One and Three Step Sparring

15 minutes Punching and Bag Work

15 minutes Kicking and Bag Work

Techniques:

Stances: More stance shifting during blocking and punching

Footwork: Glide-Drag Stepping during forward and backward motion

Blocking: Begin with One and work up to Three Step prearranged Sparring against straight punches and kicks

Punching: Begin with single punches and work up to three punch combinations on the heavy bag, working for power and fluidity

Kicking: Begin with single kicks and work up to two opposite-leg combination kicks, then two same-leg kicks as outlined in the Kicking Section

4th Session:

15 minutes Stretching and Warm Up Exercises

15 minutes Stances and Footwork

30 minutes Integrating One Punch-One Kick Combinations on the Heavy Bag

15 minutes Blocking in One through Five Step Sparring

15 minutes Kick-Punch Combinations in One and Two Step Sparring

Techniques:

Stances: Review three basic stances (Fighting, Front, Back) and stance shifting; introduce linear movement and moving from a kick into a new stance

Footwork: Linear movement in sparring

Hand-Foot Combinations: Some examples are lead leg front kick-lunge punch; lead punch/rear leg front kick; rear leg side kick-reverse punch

Blocking: Begin with One Step prearranged and work up to Five Step using the hand-foot combinations for offense

Hand-Foot Combinations in Sparring: One to Five Step prearranged Sparring using hand-foot combinations in offense and for the counter

5th Session:

15 minutes Stretching and Warm Up Exercises

15 minutes Stances and Footwork

30 minutes Integrating Hand-Foot-Hand Combinations on Heavy Bag

15 minutes Blocking in One to Five Step Sparring

15 minutes Hand-Foot-Hand Combinations in One to Three Step Sparring

Techniques:

Stances: Retreating from stance to stance in the three basic stances, stance shifting

Footwork: Linear movement going backward

Hand-Foot-Hand Combinations: Some examples are lead punch/lead leg front kick/reverse punch; lead punch/reverse leg front kick/lunge punch; work for power on the heavy bag

Blocking: Use the hand-foot-hand combinations for offense and counterattack in One through Five Step Sparring

Hand-Foot-Hand Combinations: Begin with One Step and work up to Three Step prearranged Sparring using the combinations you have worked on

6th Session:

15 minutes Stretching and Warm Up Exercises

15 minutes Stances and Footwork

30 minutes Advanced Thrusts

15 minutes Advanced Blocks

15 minutes Advanced Kicks

Techniques:

Stances: Introduction to the Straddle and Angular stances

Footwork: Moving to all points in the Straddle and Angular stances

Advanced Thrusts: Introduction to the Spear Hand Thrust, the Middle Single Knuckle Fist Thrust, and the Palm Heel Thrust

Advanced Kicks: Introduction to the Round Kick, the Outer Crescent Kick and the Inner Crescent Kick

Advanced Blocks: Introduction to the Outer Parry, Inner Parry and the Low Level Parry

7th Session:

15 minutes Stretching and Warm Up Exercises

15 minutes Stances and Footwork

30 minutes Kicking on the Heavy Bag

15 minutes Blocks

15 minutes Straight Thrusts

Techniques:

Stances: Stance shifting from basics to Straddle and Angular

Footwork: Angular stepping

Kicking: Concentrate on power kicking at the heavy bag with advanced kicks

Blocking: One Step prearranged Sparring using only parries against straight thrusts

Straight Thrusts: Begin integrating the advanced thrusts with the straight punches in combinations

8th Session:

15 minutes Stretching and Warm Up Exercises

15 minutes Stances and Footwork

30 minutes Blocking

15 minutes Kicking

15 minutes Thrusts

Techniques:

Stances: Walking the Mountain as described in the Stance Training Section

Footwork: Integral with Walking the Mountain

Blocking: One through Three Step prearranged Sparring against straight thrusts and kicks using parries only; work on Straddle and Angular stance applications in evading blows as well

Kicking: Opposite leg combination kicks on the heavy bag; for example, lead leg front snap/reverse leg round kick; front leg round kick/rear leg round kick

Thrusts: One Step prearranged Sparring using punch-thrust combination to counter; work on stance shifting; use parries

9th Session:

15 minutes Stretching and Warm Up Exercises

15 minutes Walking the Mountain

30 minutes Thrusts

15 minutes Blocking

15 minutes Kicking

Techniques:

Thrusts: One through Five Step Sparring, using advanced
thrusts to counter in prearranged sparring, using kicks
and thrusts to attack

Blocking: One through Five Step prearranged Sparring using
all blocks learned against kicks and thrusts

Kicking: Same leg two kick combinations on heavy bag; some
examples are rear leg outer crescent into side kick; lead
leg front kick into round kick; low level round kick into mid
or high level round kick, lead or reverse leg; work for
power on the heavy bag with them

10th Session:

15 minutes Stretching and Warm Up Exercises
15 minutes Walking the Mountain
30 minutes Basic Strikes
15 minutes Elbow Blocks
15 minutes Knee Kicks

Techniques:

Strikes: Introduction to the Hook Punch, Inverted Fist Punch,
and Ridge Hand; bag work

Elbow Blocks: Introduction to Elbow Blocks

Knee Kicks: Introduction to Knee Kicks on the heavy bag

11th Session:

15 minutes Stretching and Warm Up Exercises
15 minutes Walking the Mountain
30 minutes Blocking
15 minutes Strikes on Heavy Bag
15 minutes Kicking

Techniques:

Blocking: Introduction of Knee Blocks and jamming techniques;
One through Three Step Sparring using knee and elbow
blocks against kicks and thrusts

Striking: Basic strikes on heavy bag working on body
mechanics and power

Kicking: One Step Sparring using knee kicks as counters

12th Session:
15 minutes Stretching and Warm Up Exercises
15 minutes Walking the Mountain
30 minutes Kicking
15 minutes Blocking
15 minutes Strikes

Techniques:
Kicking: One through Three Step prearranged Sparring using hand-foot combinations and then knee kicks as finishing technique to counter

Blocking: Introduction of Scooping Blocks

Strikes: Integrating the basic strikes with straight thrusts in combination

Repeat all of the Sessions from **1** to **12** again, counting them as **Sessions 13** to **24,** concentrating on any "weak" spots you may have in the execution of your techniques. Developing proper form and power are what you want from the first 24 sessions, as well as building your endurance.

25th Session:
15 minutes Stretching and Warm Up Exercises
15 minutes Hand Conditioning or Walking the Mountain
30 minutes Sword Hand Strike
15 minutes Walking Blocks
15 minutes Break Falls

Techniques:
Sword Hand Strike: Introduction of the three methods of hitting with the Sword Hand; heavy bag work

Walking Blocks: Prearranged, as described in the Blocking Section Training Methods

Break Falls: Introduction to the back and side falls; working from the kneeling position

26th Session:
15 minutes Stretching and Warm Up Exercises
15 minutes Hand Conditioning or Walking the Mountain
30 minutes Hammer Fist Strike

15 minutes One through Five Step Sparring
15 minutes Break Falls

Techniques:

Hammer Fist Strike: Introduction of the three methods of striking with the bottom fist; bag work

One through Five Step Sparring: Free form attack, blocks and counter

Break Falls: Back and side falls from the standing position after short review from kneeling position

27th Session:

15 minutes Stretching and Warm Up Exercises
15 minutes Hand Conditioning or Walking the Mountain
30 minutes Backfist Strike
15 minutes Break Falls
15 minutes Walking Blocks

Techniques:

Backfist Strike: Introduction to the three methods of hitting with the backfist; heavy bag work

Break Falls: Back and side falls from the standing position

Walking Blocks: Use Sword, Hammer and Backfist strikes as offense, free form blocking and evasion

28th Session:

15 minutes Stretching and Warm Up Exercises
15 minutes Hand Conditioning or Walking the Mountain
30 minutes Elbow Strikes
15 minutes One through Three Step Sparring
15 minutes Break Falls

Techniques:

Elbow Strikes: Introduction to Elbow Strikes; heavy bag work

One through Three Step Sparring: Use thrust-strike combinations to attack, free form blocking, Sword-Hammer-Backfist strikes to counter

Break Falls: Forward rolling fall from kneeling position

29th Session:

15 minutes Stretching and Warm Up Exercises
15 minutes Forearm Conditioning or Walking the Mountain
30 minutes Strikes on Heavy Bag
15 minutes Break Falls
15 minutes One through Three Step Sparring

Techniques:

Strikes: Practice all of the strikes on the heavy bag, working them in combinations of at least three, striving for power and fluidity

Break Falls: Forward rolling fall from the standing position

One through Three Step Sparring: Kick-strike-thrust combinations for offense, free form blocks, knee-elbow counters

30th Session:

15 minutes Stretching and Warm Up Exercises
15 minutes Hand Conditioning or Walking the Mountain
30 minutes One through Five Step Sparring
15 minutes Break Falls
15 minutes Combinations on Heavy Bag

Techniques:

One through Five Step Sparring: Thrust-kick-strike combinations for offense, free form blocking, thrust-kick-strike counter

Break Falls: Forward rolling, back, and side falls from standing position

Combinations on Heavy Bag: Free form hand-foot combinations on the heavy bag

31st Session:

15 minutes Stretching and Warm Up Exercises
15 minutes Forearm Conditioning or Walking the Mountain
30 minutes Free Style Blocking
15 minutes Break Falls
15 minutes Foot Sweeps

Techniques:

Free Style Blocking: As described in the Blocking Section Training Methods

Break Falls: Forward fall from kneeling position

Foot Sweeps: Introduction to side and hooking foot sweeps

32nd Session:

    15 minutes Stretching and Warm Up Exercises
    15 minutes Hand Conditioning or Walking the Mountain
    30 minutes Grappling
    15 minutes Break Falls
    15 minutes One through Three Step Sparring

Techniques:

Grappling: Introduction to the Outer Reaping Throw and the finishing techniques; review both foot sweeps

Break Falls: Forward fall from standing position

One through Three Step Sparring: Linear attacks, free form blocking, free form counter, end the set with a foot sweep or outer reap and apply finishing techniques

33rd Session:

    15 minutes Stretching and Warm Up Exercises
    15 minutes Forearm Conditioning or Walking the Mountain
    30 minutes Grappling
    15 minutes Break Falls
    15 minutes One through Three Step Sparring

Techniques:

Grappling: Introduction to the Inner Reaping Throw and the rear body drop throw

Break Falls: Review of forward and forward rolling falls; practice by diving over low objects

One through Three Step Sparring: Linear attacks, free style blocking, free style counter, end the sets with either an inner reap or a rear body drop throw

34th Session:

    15 minutes Stretching and Warm Up Exercises
    15 minutes Forearm Conditioning or Walking the Mountain
    30 minutes Grappling
    15 minutes One through Three Step Sparring
    15 minutes Mixed Training Sets

Techniques:

Stances: Introduction to the body drop throw and shoulder throw

One through Three Step Sparring: Linear attacks, free form blocking, free form counter, end the sets with either a body drop throw or a shoulder throw and finishing technique

Mixed Training Sets: Prearranged self-defense sets from Chapter Six

35th Session:

15 minutes Stretching and Warm Up Exercises
15 minutes Hand Conditioning or Walking the Mountain
30 minutes Grappling
15 minutes One through Three Step Sparring
15 minutes Mixed Training Sets

Techniques:

Grappling: Review all throws for form and power

One through Three Step Sparring: Free form attack, free form blocks and counter, end each set with a different throw and finishing technique

Mixed Training Sets: More sets from Chapter Six

36th Session:

15 minutes Stretching and Warm Up Exercises
15 minutes Forearm Conditioning or Walking the Mountain
30 minutes One through Five Step Sparring
15 minutes Mixed Training Sets
15 minutes Free Sparring

Techniques:

One through Five Step Sparring: Free form offense, blocks and counters, ending each set with a different throw and finishing technique

Mixed Training Sets: More sets from Chapter Six, including defense against throws

Free Sparring: Totally free form light or no contact fighting where you may use any technique at any given time. Begin at slow to medium speed using full power blows that are well focused so that they stop just short of making contact with your opponent's vital striking points. If you score a clean blow on your opponent, or he one on you, it is important for you to recognize that and not treat the blow as if it did not happen. This is essential for your training skills.

Repeat **Sessions 25** to **30** for **Sessions 37** to **48.** When you have done this return to **Session 1** and go through the entire sequence again, adding in more mixed training sets of your own, devising as you go. Having gone through this whole routine twice, you should be easily able to defend yourself against any kind of physical or mental aggression. It takes a good deal of practice to gain real mastery over a martial art; this training schedule is designed to make you competent and skilled in a short time. Adhere to it and you will be.

Bibliography

The works listed here are to aid you in finding further truths about the martial arts in general and in researching facts presented in this work. Most of the works listed here were authored by masters, men that have truly internalized the lessons of their particular arts and have viewed those arts from many angles. They are able to clearly explain the essence of combative methods to their readers, in both the traditional and modern sense. They also show the reader how to carry the lessons learned in the martial arts school into one's every day life so that he becomes truly one with the art. There are many martial arts, but all of them lead to the same goal: physical and mental health.

Philosophy and History:
Zen in the Martial Arts by Joe Hyams
A Book of Five Rings by Musashi Miyamoto
The Karate Experience: A Way of Life by Randall Hassell
Karate-do Kyohon by Funakoshi Gichin
Lifetide by Lyall Watson
Heimskringla by Snorri Sturluson

Techniques and Training:
Karate, the Art of Empty Hand Fighting by Hidetaka Nishiyama
Foot Throws for Karate, Judo, and Self-Defense by Hayward Nishioka
A Guide to Martial Arts Training with Equipment by Dan Inosanto
Karate Kinematics and Dynamics by Dr. Lester Ingber
Medical Implications of Karate Blows by Brian Adams
Gray's Anatomy

Other Books by Alpha Publications

☐ **WAR WITH EMPTY HANDS, Self-Defense Against Aggression**
by Lenox Cramer
Over 10,000 copies in print!
For Beginner to Advanced.
5½ × 8½, 209 pp., striking charts, 73 photos, illus. **$16.95**

☐ **WAR WITH EMPTY HANDS** *Supplement One,* **Advanced Training**
by Lenox Cramer
Explains the mind in martial arts, weight training, how
women can defend themselves.
5½ × 8½, 92 pp., 42 photos **$10.00**

☐ **WAR WITH EMPTY HANDS** *Supplement Two,* **Field Craft**
by Lenox Cramer
Not for the squeamish! Hardcore combat techniques as
taught to anti-terrorism soldiers.
5½ × 8½, 80 pp., illus. **$10.00**

☐ **THE ULTIMATE WEAPON**
by Marco Lala
State-of-the-art martial arts training methods, exercises and
improvised equipment that works!
6 × 9, 80 pp., photos, illus. **$14.95**

☐ **PHENOMENAL ENDURANCE TRAINING**
by Marco Lala
Explosive fighting power is yours! Weekly training
schedules included for beginner to advanced.
8½ × 11, 25 pp., photos **$9.95**

☐ **HOW TO KNOCK OUT ANY ATTACKER WITHIN SECONDS**
by Marco Lala
Exciting new instructional video. Reveals the *fastest, most
effective* way to become a superior fighter!
60 minutes, color, VHS Video Only **$49.95**

☐ **ALPHA Book Catalog**
Hundreds of Titles Available!
Free With Order **$1.00**

Order Form

Title	Price	Qty.	Total
1. War With Empty Hands	$16.95		
2. War With . . . Hands — Advanced Training	$10.00		
3. War With . . . Hands — Field Craft	$10.00		
4. The Ultimate Weapon	$14.95		
5. Phenomenal Endurance Training	$9.95		
6. How To . . . Attacker Within Seconds	$49.95		
7. Book Catalog only (free with order)	$ 1.00		
OHIO Residents add 5½% Sales Tax **SUBTOTAL**			
SHIPPING AND HANDLING			$3.00
TOTAL AMOUNT DUE			

Satisfaction Guaranteed!

ALPHA PUBLICATIONS of Ohio
P.O. Box 308-A
Sharon Center, Ohio 44274

Name_____

Address_____

State_____ Zip_____

☐ Check/Money Order ☐ Visa ☐ Mastercard

Card # _____ Exp. Date_____

Thank you for your order!

NOTES

NOTES